FLAGSHIP HISTORYMAKERS

DISRAELI

MARY DICKEN

An imprint of HarperCollins*Publishers*

Contents

Why do historians differ?

THE purpose of the Flagship Historymakers series is to explore the main debates surrounding a number of key individuals in British, European and American History.

Each book begins with a chronology of the significant events in the life of the particular individual, and an outline of the person's career. The book then examines in greater detail three of the most important and controversial issues in the life of the individual – issues which continue to attract differing views from historians, and which feature prominently in examination syllabuses in A-level History and beyond.

Each of these issue sections provides students with an overview of the main arguments put forward by historians. By posing key questions, these sections aim to help students to think through the areas of debate and to form their own judgements on the evidence. It is important, therefore, for students to understand why historians differ in their views on past events and, in particular, on the role of individuals in past events.

The study of history is an ongoing debate about events in the past. Although factual evidence is the essential ingredient of history, it is the *interpretation* of factual evidence that forms the basis for historical debate. The study of how and why historians differ in their various interpretations is termed 'historiography'.

Historical debate can occur for a wide variety of reasons.

Insufficient evidence

In some cases there is insufficient evidence to provide a definitive conclusion. In attempting to 'fill the gaps' where factual evidence is unavailable, historians use their professional judgement to make 'informed comments' about the past.

New evidence

As new evidence comes to light, an historian today may have more information on which to base judgements than historians in the past. For instance, a major source of information about 19th-century political history is the Public Record Office (PRO) in Kew, London. Some of the information held at the PRO has remained confidential for up to 100 years. Therefore, it is only recently that historians have been able to analyse and assess this evidence.

A 'philosophy' of history?

Many historians have a specific view of history that will affect the way they make their historical judgements. For instance, Marxist historians – who take their view from the writings of Karl Marx, the founder of modern socialism – believe that society has always been made up of competing economic and social classes. They also place considerable importance on economic reasons behind human decision-making. Therefore, a Marxist historian looking at an historical issue may take a completely different viewpoint to a non-Marxist historian.

The role of the individual

Some historians have seen past history as being largely moulded by the acts of specific individuals. Disraeli, Gladstone and Lord Palmerston are seen as individuals whose personality and beliefs changed the course of nineteenth-century British history. Other historians have tended to play down the role of the individuals; instead, they highlight the importance of more general social, economic and political change. Rather than seeing Joseph Chamberlain as an individual who changed the course of political history, these historians tend to see him as representing the views of a broader group of individuals, such as the industrial middle class of late Victorian Britain.

Placing different emphasis on the same historical evidence

Even if historians do not possess different philosophies of history or place different emphasis on the role of the individual, it is still possible for them to disagree in one very important way. This is that they may place different emphases on aspects of the same factual evidence. As a result, History should be seen as a subject that encourages debate about the past, based on historical evidence.

Historians will always differ

Historical debate is, in its nature, continuous. What today may be an accepted view about a past event may well change in the future, as the debate continues.

Timeline: Disraeli's life

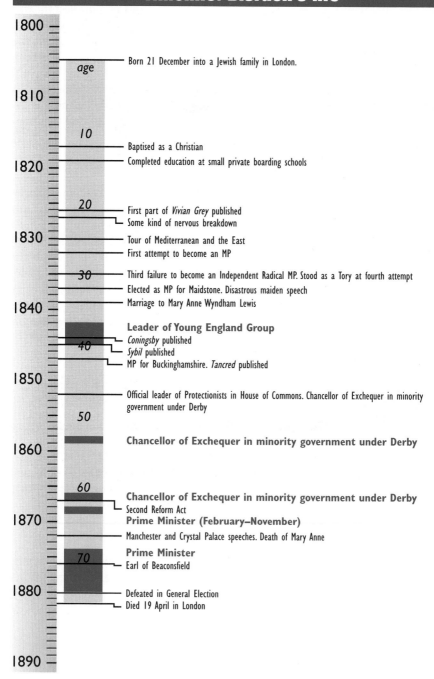

1800

age

Born 21 December into a Jewish family in London.

1810

10

Baptised as a Christian

Completed education at small private boarding schools

1820

20

First part of *Vivian Grey* published

Some kind of nervous breakdown

1830

Tour of Mediterranean and the East

First attempt to become an MP

30

Third failure to become an Independent Radical MP. Stood as a Tory at fourth attempt

Elected as MP for Maidstone. Disastrous maiden speech

Marriage to Mary Anne Wyndham Lewis

1840

Leader of Young England Group

40

Coningsby published

Sybil published

MP for Buckinghamshire. *Tancred* published

1850

Official leader of Protectionists in House of Commons. Chancellor of Exchequer in minority government under Derby

50

Chancellor of Exchequer in minority government under Derby

1860

60

Chancellor of Exchequer in minority government under Derby

Second Reform Act

Prime Minister (February–November)

1870

Manchester and Crystal Palace speeches. Death of Mary Anne

Prime Minister

70

Earl of Beaconsfield

1880

Defeated in General Election

Died 19 April in London

1890

Benjamin Disraeli (1804–81) Conservative Prime Minister and novelist.

Disraeli: a brief biography

How did he make history?

Benjamin Disraeli (1804–81) has fascinated and repelled from his own time to the present day. At first sight his role was slight: Chancellor of the Exchequer in three short lived minority governments and Prime Minister for a few months in 1868 and then again at the end if his life. However, he was at the centre of key Victorian events in 1846, 1867 and 1875–8. To many he will always be the unprincipled adventurer, supremely assured of his own genius, ready to sacrifice any consistency in his ideas in order to achieve power. His chief accomplishment was to become Prime Minister in the face of the barriers he had to surmount, such as his education and his background. He is also promoted as the saviour of the Conservative Party, defender of the aristocracy, the initiator of real social reform, the upholder of British interests abroad and the originator of the imperialist ideal. He has been credited with saving the monarchy by enticing **Queen Victoria** back into public life after the death of Albert. He was a superb Parliamentary orator, after a false start, known for his wit and perception. He had an unusual gift in that he could bring a sense of romance and excitement to politics and even into the Conservative Party. One of his contemporaries summed up Disraeli's career as 'failure, failure, failure, partial success, renewed failure, ultimate and complete victory'.

Queen Victoria (1819–1901)
Became monarch in 1837 aged 18. She married Albert of Saxe-Coburg in 1840 and was much influenced by him in politics. She favoured Peel and was appalled by Disraeli's attacks on him. But her views mellowed and in 1861, the Disraelis were entertained at Windsor. Disraeli's public tribute to Prince Albert comforted Victoria when Albert died suddenly in 1861. When he became Prime Minister, his charm and his entertaining letters won her over completely and she became his 'faery'. This was in strong contrast with Gladstone whom the Queen loathed.

Disraeli's early life

Disraeli's family was Jewish, and lived near Grays Inn in London. His father Isaac had inherited money and was known in literary circles for his books such as *The Curiosities of Literature* published in 1791. The children were baptised as Christians, Benjamin in 1817. Without this he could not have become a Member of Parliament, as until 1858, Jews could not sit as MPs as they could not take the Parliamentary Oath. Unlike other political figures of the day, Disraeli did not go to a good public school but to a Dame's School in Islington, a boarding school in Blackheath and then another boarding school, Higham Hall in Essex, which he left in 1819 when he was 15. He did not, again unusually, proceed to Oxford or Cambridge. Unwise speculation landed him with serious debts as a young man from which he did not escape until he was 60.

Sir Robert Peel (1788–1850)
From a background very similar to Gladstone, Peel was an MP at 21 and served in the Tory governments of the 1820s. In 1834 in his Tamworth Manifesto he outlined a new philosophy for his party to conserve what was good and to reform what was not. His Free Trade budgets carried out this aim in his ministry of 1841–6, but the Irish Famine led him to repeal the Corn Laws and split his party as he had done previously in 1829 over Catholic Emancipation. He died in 1850 after a fall from his horse.

Young England Group: a small group of aristocrats yearning for the feudal paternalism of the past, but dominated by Disraeli. The group received far more publicity than its numbers warranted and their criticisms of Peel, while remaining Tories, kept them in the public eye.

He began to write novels, partly as a result of work on political pamphlets for John Murray, his father's publisher, and partly inspired by the current fashion for 'silver fork fiction' which focused on high society. His first novel, *Vivian Grey*, which was published in two parts in 1826–7 was a failure of which even he was later ashamed. The production of fiction was not seen as a worthy occupation for a politician. Between 1827 and 1830, his health broke down. His father rented a house for him to recover at Bradenham in Buckinghamshire. In 1830–1 he travelled to Europe and the Middle East where his love of the Orient was formed in his 'repose on luxurious Ottomans' and his enjoyment of being able to 'smoke superb pipes' and 'daily to indulge in the luxuries of a bath'.

A career in politics

He continued to write, publishing more novels in 1828, 1831, 1833, 1836 and 1837. The passing of the Reform Bill in 1832, led Disraeli to consider a political career, not as a Tory like his father, but as a Radical. He was a candidate at High Wycombe in 1832 when he was 28. This was the first of his repeated efforts to secure election to the House of Commons. This again marks a contrast with most of the leading politicians of his day. His eventual success in politics came about when his mistress Henrietta Sykes introduced him to Lord Lyndhurst, an influential Conservative, and in 1837, aged 33, he became one of the members for Maidstone, grateful that MPs could not be arrested for debt.

His career did not, even then, take off. His maiden speech in 1837 was a disaster, **Sir Robert Peel** refused him a place in his government in 1841 and Disraeli with his **Young England Group** became increasingly critical of Peel. His Jewishness made him a target of anti-semitism and his nickname 'Dizzy' was not entirely affectionate. In 1839 he married **Mary Anne Lewis**, a wealthy widow and at the age of 55, 12 years his senior. Despite the age difference, it was a happy relationship. There were no children. In 1844–7, he published his best known novels *Sybil, Coningsby* and *Tancred*.

Mary Anne Lewis (1792–1872)
Her husband Wyndham Lewis was the other MP for Maidstone. He died suddenly in 1838. It was highly convenient for Disraeli to marry her, because of her wealth, but he seems to have loved her sincerely, referring to her as a perfect wife. She suffered from stomach cancer and her death devastated Disraeli who claimed he had not been separated from her for 33 years and never had a moment of dullness in her society.

Corn Laws: were passed in 1815 to protect English farmers from cheap foreign corn flooding the market. They had been modified with no apparent negative effects on agriculture. The Irish famine of 1845 necessitated the import of cheap corn.

In 1846, the repeal of the **Corn Laws** gave Disraeli his opportunity, and he seized his chance to express the outrage of many Conservatives at Peel's betrayal of their party. But despite his public prominence, Disraeli was further than ever from power. For the next 20 years, British politics were dominated by Whig/Liberal administrations. Disraeli was mistrusted by many and only became a landed gentleman when the Bentinck family helped him to buy Hughenden Manor in Buckinghamshire. It was 1852, when he was 48, before he was recognised as official leader of the Protectionists in the House of Commons. He then became Chancellor of the Exchequer in the minority government under Derby.

Prime Minister at last

The government formed in 1866 was probably the last chance for Disraeli, now aged 62, to secure the success he craved. In a series of amazing manoeuvres, he succeeded in passing the 1867 Parliamentary Reform Act. In addition the Government passed successful social reforms such as a Factory Act, a Poor Law Act and a Public Health Act and intervened in Abyssinia. In 1868, Derby

Disraeli reaching the top of the political 'greasy pole' in this 1868 cartoon. The caption reads 'At last'.

Understanding Disraeli

Disraeli's mercurial (changeable) character makes it hard to understand him, but it is believed he had the following fundamental characteristics:

- An **exaggerated respect for the aristocracy** and their role in government as the class to which he could never quite belong.

- A **firm, lasting will** which propelled him to power.

- A **staunch defence of Britain's imperial interests** along with personal concern with the Orient and the eastern Mediterranean.

- A **mastery of ideas** accompanied by a desire not to be involved in detail, most marked when he was Prime Minister.

- A **respect for the monarchy** leading to his special relationship with Queen Victoria.

- **Brilliance as a Parliamentary orator and tactician**, most clearly seen in the passing of the 1867 Reform Act.

- An **opportunism** exemplified by his readiness to encourage social reform or economic policies such as Protection when these helped to increase his support, and to abandon them at will.

- A **readiness to humiliate and defeat Gladstone**.

- A **desire to see Britain respected in Europe** in the traditions of Palmerston.

- A **love of the social round** where his conversational brilliance could be displayed at dinner parties and receptions.

- A **love of female company** from his sister Sarah, to Henrietta Sykes, to Mary Anne and, after her death, to Anne Countess of Chesterfield and Selina Countess of Bradford. He wrote constantly to women, including the Queen, providing much insight into the political process for modern readers.

- An **ability to publish novels** over a 50 year period which provide many clues to his view of events of his own time and the development of his philosophy.

'He is a self-made man, and worships his creator'
John Bright, the leading Liberal, on Disraeli

William Ewart Gladstone (1809–98)
A strong contrast with and rival to Disraeli from a conventional middle class background, educated at Eton and Oxford, he was given office by Peel who was his hero and became devoted to Free Trade. He was loyal to Peel in 1846 and after some wavering, joined the Liberal Party, becoming its leader in 1867 and Prime Minister in 1868–74. His main interests lay in sound finance, promotion of opportunity for all, a moral foreign policy and a solution to the Irish problem. He clashed frequently with Disraeli, notably over foreign policy. He was Prime Minister for three more ministries in 1880–5, 1886 and 1892–4.

resigned and Disraeli was Prime Minister at last. He was 64. 'Yes', said Disraeli to his friends when he became Prime Minister, 'I have climbed to the top of the greasy pole'. The implied comparison of politics with a fairground side show suggests it was a game for Disraeli; an unusual impression in a period where politics was a serious business. His elation was short lived as he slid down the greasy pole again after the Conservative defeat in the 1868 election.

The formation of **Gladstone**'s Liberal Ministry, with a strong programme, was a real challenge for a man in his late 60s. Disraeli's leadership of his party came close to being undermined by Lord Cairns and other leading Conservatives who favoured the fifteenth Earl of Derby as leader. In speeches at the Free Trade Hall, Manchester and the Crystal Palace in London in 1872, Disraeli redefined Conservatism. He developed the essential themes of patriotism, the empire, loyalty to church and monarch and the need to improve public health and working and living conditions. In opposition he turned again to writing, publishing *Lothair* in 1870 when he was 66.

Partly as a result of improvements in the organisation of the Conservative Party, and partly because of the unpopularity of some of the Liberal measures, in 1874 Disraeli won the election, giving the Conservatives their first overall Parliamentary majority since 1846. However, Disraeli was 70 in 1874 and not in good health. His wife, Mary Anne had died in December 1872 and was much mourned by Disraeli. His leadership was limited and the initiative for legislation passed to ministers like Richard Cross, the Home Secretary.

In foreign affairs, he exerted himself more. The purchase of the Suez Canal shares in 1875 was very much his policy, and he made the most of his success. In 1876, he was largely responsible for making the Queen Empress of India and, in return, according to some critics, he became Earl of Beaconsfield, and moved to the more exalted atmosphere of the House of Lords. The eruption of the

Eastern Question:
Britain wished to prevent the collapse of the Turkish Empire in order to avoid Russian expansion into the Mediterranean or India as this would threaten the British Empire.

Eastern Question brought Gladstone out of retirement and sparked an increasingly hostile exchange between the two. Disraeli triumphed at the Congress of Berlin in 1878, notably on the dinner party circuit showing amazing stamina for a man of 74 suffering from gout and asthma, and achieved 'Peace with Honour'. Disasters in Afghanistan and South Africa, attacked by Gladstone as Beaconsfieldism, did not enhance Disraeli's reputation. An agricultural and industrial depression added to his unpopularity. In 1880, the Conservatives were defeated, much to the dismay of the Queen.

Disraeli's final years

He now completed his last novel *Endymion* for which the publisher Longman paid him £10 000. It included a brief pen portrait of Bismarck whom he had met at the Congress of Berlin. He was working on a further novel at his death in which the main character was clearly based on Gladstone. In March 1881 Disraeli caught a chill and never recovered, dying on 19 April. The Queen was overwhelmed: 'I can scarcely see for my fast falling tears', she wrote, and at Disraeli's funeral she famously sent 'His favourite flowers from Osborne' as a tribute of her affection. The outsider had become a fully accepted part of English society and associated, however unlikely it may appear, with the pale petals of the primrose.

Disraeli in 1875, indulging in one of his favourite pastimes.

1

How did Disraeli become leader of the Conservative Party?

Was his opposition to Peel in 1846 a question of principle or opportunism?

Did his experience in government in 1852 and 1858–9 advance his prospects?

Did he advance his career after the fall of Peel in 1846?

Did the passing of the Second Reform Act in 1867 help to bring him to power?

Framework of events

1846	Repeal of the Corn Laws. Resignation of Peel
1847	Disraeli MP for Buckinghamshire
1848	Bentinck resigned as Protectionist Conservative leader in the House of Commons and later died
1849	Disraeli leader in the Commons of Protectionist Conservatives, in practice if not in name
1852	Death of Peel. Tories the largest group after the election but without a majority
1852	First Derby-Dizzy Government but defeated on Disraeli's budget
1853	Aberdeen Coalition Government of Whigs and Peelites formed
1854–6	Crimean War
1855	Resignation of Aberdeen. Palmerston Prime Minister
1855	General Election. Majority for Palmerston. Liberal Government
1858	Defeat for Palmerston. Second Derby-Dizzy Government
1859	Conservative Reform Bill defeated
1859	Formation of Liberal Party
1859	General Election. Palmerston Prime Minister. Liberal Government
1865	General Election. Palmerston continued as Prime Minister but died
1865	Lord John Russell Prime Minister. Liberal Government
1866	Russell's Reform Bill defeated. Third Derby-Dizzy Government
1867	Second Reform Bill passed
1868	Derby resigned. Disraeli Prime Minister
1868	General Election. Liberal victory

ISTORIANS such as Edgar Feuchtwanger (*Disraeli*, 2000) have stressed how unlikely it was that Disraeli would rise to lead the Conservative Party, let alone be Prime Minister, since he did not 'share much of the prevailing ethos of the era'. Feuchtwanger further argues that although other successful Victorians were outsiders, none of them were 'outsiders in as many ways as Disraeli was'. Not only was Disraeli a Jew, but he had no public school or university background and so had made none of the useful social contacts most of the ruling classes formed in their early years. He was convinced he was a genius but as historian Ian Machin (*Disraeli*, 1995) suggests, he was uncertain as to whether his chosen field would be journalism, fiction, poetry or politics.

Once he settled on politics, his rise was fascinating because of 'the exceptionally long distance he had to rise in order to get where he did'. Historian Terry Jenkins (*Disraeli and Victorian Conservatism*, 1996) is less inclined to the view that Disraeli was necessarily set apart since his family was from the prosperous middle classes. He suggests that Disraeli's appearance 'black locks of hair, a pale complexion and dark eyes' together with the way he was treated at school for his Jewishness, led him to feel isolated and that he was an outsider. Historian Lord Blake (*Disraeli*, 1966) concurs. Disraeli was 'born into a family neither obscure, undistinguished nor poor' but he 'suffered from a potentially fatal handicap. He was a Jew'. All these historians agree that the events in 1846 gave Disraeli a 'wonderful, indeed a unique opportunity'.

Was Disraeli's opposition to Peel in 1846 a question of principle or opportunism?

In 1841, both Disraeli and his wife wrote to Sir Robert Peel asking that Disraeli might find a place in the new administration. Peel's reply gave Disraeli some hope that he could be involved in the future.

Factory Act 1844: this reduced the maximum hours which could be worked by women and children under 18.

Protection: a system whereby tariffs on foreign goods entering the country protected the market for home produced goods.

The principled attack on Peel

Disraeli supported Peel in 1842 in some relaxation of the Corn Laws and in 1844 over Ireland. He backed the **Factory Act of 1844**, but he was unable to support the repeal of the Corn Laws and saw Peel's desertion of **Protection** as a betrayal of the agricultural interest, the backbone of the party. 'Let men stand by the principles by which they rise', he asserted. In this version of events, Disraeli and

The contrast between Gladstone (right) and Disraeli (below) as young politicians.

Lord George Bentinck (1802–48)
Bentinck was the son of the Duke of Portland, an MP since 1828 but spoke rarely. Celebrated for his racing successes, he first came into contact with Disraeli in 1846. He saw Peel as a traitor. He died suddenly in 1848.

Anti-Corn Law League: founded in 1839 by Radical John Bright and Liberal Richard Cobden. As a single issue pressure group, it was highly successful and achieved its end in 1846 with the repeal of the Corn Laws.

Palmerstonian Whigs: an aristocratic political group who had favoured Parliamentary reform in 1832 but were reluctant to agree to more reform. Palmerston exemplified their outlook.

Lord George Bentinck who had declared he 'never could be guilty of double dealing with the farmers of England, of swindling our opponents, deceiving our friends, or betraying our constituents' are the principled heroes against the turncoat Peel. Given that 242 former supporters of Peel voted against him in 1846, there is some justification for this interpretation.

The historian Lord Blake writes that 'it is hard to overstate the bitterness and fury which Peel's decision had provoked'. Even the former Prime Minister, Lord Melbourne, himself known as a cynical politician, exclaimed to the Queen, 'Ma'am it's a damned dishonest act'. Historian John Walton (*Disraeli,* 1990) supports this view arguing that Disraeli attacked Peel for 'changing his policy without consulting the electorate or listening to the views of his supporters' and not because he was defending agricultural Protection.

The historian, Ian Machin has also stressed that there was strong public opinion in the constituencies in reaction against the **Anti-Corn Law League**. Hence, although the vigour of Disraeli's attacks was a vital part of the anti-Peel campaign, it was not the sole cause of Peel's downfall.

Seizing the opportunity

Disraeli seized his chance with vigour. In 1836, he had described Peel as a man of 'splendid talents and spotless character', but by 1845, Peel was 'without imagination or any inspiring qualities'. Historian Edgar Feuchtwanger points out that Disraeli soon 'embarked upon a difficult campaign to wean the party from Protection' and claimed he had never been a convinced Protectionist. He abandoned the policy later and in the 1870s refused to allow the farmers protection against American imports. This indicates that Disraeli's main object in 1846 was the removal of Peel and the promotion of himself: a clear case of seizing the opportunity. It has even been suggested that at one point, Disraeli was ready to work with the **Palmerstonian Whigs** thus hardly demonstrating party loyalty.

Principle or opportunism?

One of the weaknesses of Disraeli's line of argument which was eventually taken up by Peel, was that he had asked for office in 1841. Disraeli maintained 'nothing of the kind ever occurred' and was fortunate Peel did not produce his 1841 letter. Even the historian William Flavelle Monypenny, one of Disraeli's admirers admits he 'was no moral hero' but also asserts that Disraeli diverged from Peel

Landmark Study The book that changed people's views

W.L. Monypenny and G.E. Buckle, *The Life of Benjamin Disraeli, Earl of Beaconsfield,* (John Murray, 1910–20)

This massive six volume work with over 1 million words, is based largely on the papers left by Disraeli to Montagu Corry (later Lord Rowton) his secretary. It includes a great many extracts from Disraeli's letters and speeches and is a major source for anyone studying Disraeli. But this is, of course, evidence from the man himself. The first two volumes were written by Monypenny, a journalist on the *Times,* and the last four by Buckle who had recently left the post of Editor of the *Times.* They saw the modern Conservative Party as Disraeli's creation and also emphasise his 'complex character and genius'. Monypenny believed that 'mystery was the essence of the man'. To Buckle he was 'a grand, magnificent figure, standing solitary, towering above his contemporaries'. The book is notably favourable to Disraeli but not uncritical. It omits references to his sexual and financial adventures. Robert Blake in 1966 used Monypenny and Buckle extensively in his biography but modified some of the conclusions about Disraeli.

on 'a clear question of principle and under pressure from his constituents'.

Disraeli asserted that the party should be the main consideration for a politician 'For it is only by maintaining the independence of party that you can maintain the integrity of public men and the power and influence of Parliament itself'. He could argue that Peel had given no hint to his party that he was thinking of such a radical step as repeal of the Corn Laws. When Disraeli first spoke against repeal, he was a lone voice. It was unlikely that he would be acceptable as a Conservative leader in a party of landed squires, which again suggests he was not being opportunist. On the other hand, Disraeli had taken up a variety of causes: Radicalism; Peelite Conservatism; Young England and now the defence of the English country gentlemen, thus making him look like an opportunist.

Did Disraeli advance his career after the fall of Peel in 1846?

The Conservatives were not to enjoy a further electoral triumph until 1874, so, at first sight, Disraeli seems to have ruined his chances, perhaps merely to have a spiteful revenge on a man who had not appeared to appreciate his remarkable qualities. Moreover, the repeal of the Corn Laws, contrary to his prophecies, had not ruined agriculture.

Lord Edward Stanley (1799–1869)

Stanley (Derby) was a Whig MP 1820–44. In 1844, he became a member of the House of Lords at his own request. He was recognised as leader of the Protectionists in 1846 and hence led the Conservatives after the split. In 1851 he became the fourteenth Earl of Derby. He was Prime Minister three times; in 1852, 1858–9 and 1866–8.

Disraeli and Derby

The Conservative Party was now led by **Lord Stanley** (Derby) in the House of Lords who remained its 'undisputed master' and by Bentinck in the House of Commons. Bentinck proved an embarrassing leader and it was said that when he attacked the Government, he was similar to 'a wild animal at feeding time'. In 1847, both Disraeli and Bentinck supported the bill to allow Jewish MPs to delete the words 'on the true faith of a Christian' from the Parliamentary Oath, which made Bentinck unacceptable to the rank and file Conservatives. In both their cases this was one example of genuine belief and feeling.

When Bentinck resigned (in 1848), Derby was unwilling to see Disraeli in his place, partly because he was a non-aristocrat in a very aristocratic party. Derby wanted a former Chancellor of the Exchequer, J.C. Herries, as Leader in the commons, but Disraeli refused to serve under him. Derby then suggested a trio of Herries, Disraeli and the Marquess of Granby. In 1852, Granby resigned (and later became Duke of Rutland) and Disraeli was acknowledged as the sole leader of the Commons, although he had in practice been leader since 1849.

The historian Ian Machin considers Disraeli benefited from the fall of Peel. For one thing, although left in the political wilderness, he was now clearly the most promising Conservative MP. The historian Terry Jenkins argues 'subsequent events helped to catapult Disraeli into a position of authority which he could never have expected to achieve so quickly if at all'. He had demonstrated both oratorical and organising abilities in 1846, bearing out his own words when his maiden speech had been howled down; 'I shall sit down now but the time will come when you will hear me'.

Disraeli's rise to power

Disraeli moved rapidly from the back benches of the Government party to the front benches as leader of a large opposition party. He was also ready to give up Protection and in time, to support Parliamentary reform and social measures, in fact, in the end, to come closer to the party of Peel. Disraeli overcame many of the prejudices of the Protectionist MPs. In 1830, he had appeared in green velvet trousers, a canary coloured waistcoat, silver buckles, lace at his wrists and his hair in ringlets. On another occasion, his light blue trousers and black stockings with red stripes caused a sensation (which was his intention). In 1847 he wore a sober black or brown suit, acquired his own country estate at Hughenden

Manor in Buckinghamshire and was able to sit as MP for Buckinghamshire. This, historian Ian Machin argues, gave him the land-owning background he needed to become acceptable to the Protectionists as a leader.

When Bentinck died of a heart attack in 1848, Disraeli began work on a biography of his friend which seemed a nobler undertaking than works of fiction. He was also by now, as historian Paul Adelman suggests (*Gladstone, Disraeli and later Victorian Politics,* 1970) the 'outstanding Parliamentarian' on the Tory side, the best debater and the 'cleverest man' they possessed. But, in the final outcome, of greatest significance was the absence from the Conservative Party of William Gladstone. Gladstone had been out of Parliament in 1846 and so unable to defend his hero Peel. Gladstone had rejoined Peel's government in 1845 and in accordance with the rules of the day, had to seek re-election. His patron, the Duke of Newcastle, refused to support his **Free Trade** stance so he had to find a new seat. He returned in 1847 as MP for Oxford and joined the Peelite group. The man who had been described as 'the rising hope of those stern and unbending Tories' had already decided Disraeli was an untrustworthy adventurer. It was not yet certain that Gladstone would never return to the Conservative fold but it was unlikely and this could only be to Disraeli's advantage. Historian Angus Hawkins (*British Party Politics 1852–1886,* 1998) points out that at least the Conservative Party under Derby and Disraeli was united and cohesive, whereas the Liberals were likely to break up and fragment. Hence the Conservatives had some hope of attaining power.

Free Trade: this was the opposite of Protection, meaning tariffs on foreign goods should be abolished as far as possible.

Did Disraeli's experience in government in 1852 and 1858–9 advance his prospects?

In February 1852, the Protectionist Conservatives formed a minority government and Disraeli became Chancellor of the Exchequer. The members of the government were largely unknown and hence it was christened the 'Who? Who?' administration, this being the response of the **Duke of Wellington** to the list of names.

Duke of Wellington	Waterloo. He was Prime	was given a magnificent
(1769–1852)	Minister on two occasions,	State Funeral.
The Duke of Wellington was	1828–30 and 1834. By	
mainly known for his	1850 he was a respected	
military achievements,	elder Statesman and also	
notably the Battle of	deaf. He died in 1852 and	

Disraeli as Chancellor of the Exchequer

This was a period of instability in party politics with many changes of ministry. Historian Terry Jenkins has suggested that Disraeli's budget of 1852 was designed to appeal as widely as possible in order to attract more support for his party and thus improve its chances of survival as a government. He proposed reductions in the **Malt Tax** to help farmers, the hop duty to win over the beer drinking classes and the tea duty to help the whole nation, but a higher house tax was needed to compensate. Historian Terry Jenkins argues Disraeli was unfortunate in that he faced three former Chancellors of the Exchequer on the opposition benches. At a late stage, there were new demands for defence expenditure which reduced his room for manoeuvre, but more importantly, Disraeli's speech in defence of his budget was demolished by Gladstone for its subversive tendencies. This has been seen as Gladstone's revenge for Disraeli's attitude to Peel and marked a sharper and more personal stage in their rivalry.

Disraeli had at least now held a major office, the only one he held before he became Prime Minister. He remained indispensable to the Conservatives and had persuaded Derby to abandon Protection. On the negative side, he was accused of hypocrisy on this issue and was not, as a man constantly in debt, viewed as a suitable Chancellor even if Derby famously told him 'They give you the figures!'.

Moreover, the Queen's hostility (due to his conduct to Peel) had probably prevented him from becoming Home or Foreign Secretary, more prestigious jobs, since she regularly saw these ministers. His budget's shortcomings had been laid bare by the financial expertise of Gladstone.

Malt Tax: a tax on barley grown for malting. It was very unpopular with farmers and by halving it, Disraeli hoped to bring more land into production with more profits from growing barley and also to please all by cutting the price of beer as a result. It was seen as a favour to the farmers.

Out of power

A new coalition Government replaced the Derby-Disraeli Government in 1853. During this time out of power, Disraeli dabbled with journalism. He remained distrusted by his party and distant from Derby. According to historian Angus Hawkins he exploited the resentment and distrust between the various groups which made up the new coalition Government of **Lord Aberdeen**.

Lord Aberdeen (1784–1860)
Lord Aberdeen was a Scottish peer who had held several cabinet posts and after 1846 led the Peelites in the House of Lords. He was Prime Minister 1852–5 in a coalition Government which fell when its management of the Crimean War was criticised.

A second chance

It was not until 1858 that the Conservatives achieved power. This came about because their opponents had quarrelled among themselves as Disraeli hoped they would. No other group would join them. Gladstone was invited. Disraeli claimed 'I almost went

Lord John Russell	He held several cabinet	ministry he favoured a bold
(1792–1878)	posts and was Prime	approach to Parliamentary
Russell was a Liberal and	Minister in 1846–52 and	reform.
made Earl Russell in 1861.	1865–6. In his second	

down on my knees to him'. His dislike of Disraeli led him to decline. Gladstone was well aware that the Liberal leaders, **Lord John Russell** and Palmerston, were considerably older than Derby and Disraeli and so his hopes of leading the Liberals were more likely to materialise. Disraeli took no chances this time and his budgets were models of financial prudence proposing truly Gladstonian measures such as a reduction in income tax and the end of the duty on paper.

Mutiny: the mutiny in India began in May 1857 and was not put down until June 1858. Atrocities on both sides were common. As a result, the East India Company ended its role in Indian administration.

The main achievement of 1858 was the India Act, reshaping the Government of India after the **mutiny**. Disraeli wrote to Queen Victoria about her Indian subjects, 'the name of your Majesty ought to be impressed upon their native life'. This reflects not only Disraeli's improving relationship with the Court but also his vision of an Indian Empire. Although the ministry lasted 16, rather than ten months this time, it brought the Conservatives no nearer to real power. Derby and Disraeli were defeated in 1859 when their moderate proposals for Parliamentary reform alarmed some Conservatives but were not radical enough for the Liberals.

Church rates: paid by all for the upkeep of the Church of England buildings. Naturally nonconformists (Protestants who dissented from the Church of England) resented this.

The Liberals take over

Burials: a non-conformist grievance. They wanted the right to bury their members in parish churchyards with their own form of service which was currently not allowed.

In the 1859 Election, the conservatives won over 300 seats, but were still in a minority. Their opponents were now united as the Liberal Party with Radicals, Peelites and Whigs within it. Prospects for the Conservative Party and its leader seemed dim. Historian Ian Machin suggests 'the next six years were particularly discouraging to Disraeli's quest for power'. Angus Hawkins quotes Disraeli who said 'The leadership of hopeless opposition is a gloomy affair'. Machin also stresses that Disraeli's position as leader was still insecure. He needed to gain favour with the right wing of his party. He opposed bills to abolish **church rates** and to remedy non-conformist grievances over **burials**. He even aligned himself with traditionalist views in the current **Darwinist** debate. None of these were positions to which he held consistently. Then in 1865, Palmerston, the arch opponent of Parliamentary reform, died. This opened up a new situation with many possibilities for Disraeli. It came none too soon. Disraeli was 61.

Darwinist: Charles Darwin published the *Origins of Species* in 1859, and in 1860 his theories about evolution were attacked by Samuel Wilberforce (the Bishop of Oxford) at a public meeting.

Did the passing of the Second Reform Act in 1867 help to bring Disraeli to power?

John Stuart Mill (1806–73)
Mill was a Liberal MP briefly, but was better known as a utilitarian philosopher and an eager supporter of equality for women and respect for minorities.

Reform Union: a largely middle class group based in Manchester. It campaigned for all male ratepayers to have the vote. It was formed by John Bright, a radical Liberal who had worked to repeal the Corn Laws and was a keen supporter of Free Trade. He felt aristocratic government was inefficient.

Pale of the constitution: a metaphor used by Gladstone. The 'pale' refers to a fence, and Gladstone believed all responsible males were entitled to come into the privileged enclosed political world by having the right to vote.

The Second Reform Act in 1867 was, says Sean Lang (*Parliamentary Reform*, 1999) the result of 'a long complicated process of Parliamentary manoeuvring which had contemporaries bemused and confused'. Historian Ian Machin (*The Rise of Democracy in Britain, 1939–1918*, 2001) argues that external pressures such as the formation of the **Reform Union** in 1864 by John Bright led to the Reform Act. He adds that intellectuals, influenced by the writings of **John Stuart Mill**, had became greater supporters of Parliamentary reform.

The death of Palmerston is often seen as a defining moment in the move for reform. Hoppen (*The Mid-Victorian Generation 1846–1886*, 1998) considers that 'Gladstone was the figure around whom the events of reform gathered'. In support of this view, he refers to Gladstone's statement in May 1864 'Every man who is not presumably incapacitated by some consideration of personal unfitness or of political danger is morally entitled to come within the **pale of the constitution**'. John Walton (*The Second Reform Act*, 1983) agrees that 'the most important development might seem to be Gladstone's conversion'.

The defeat of the Liberals

This left little place for Disraeli to influence events but never the less he was able to seize the moment. As historian Terry Jenkins asserts, the 'Liberal Party's inability to maintain unity on the reform issue' was in his favour. Earl Russell as Prime Minister, strongly supported by Gladstone, introduced a moderate Reform Bill to Parliament with a £7 borough **household franchise** and a £14 **county franchise**. A group of Liberals, led by Robert Lowe and known as the **Adullamites** rejected this, and so the Conservatives were able to combine with them to defeat the Government, ensure its fall and thus come to power.

John Walton considers that the vigour with which the Liberals promoted the Reform Bill increased the opposition within their own party. He also argues that Disraeli marshalled the Conservative arguments against the detail of the Liberal proposals and persuaded

Household franchise: all male heads of households, whether owners or tenants, could vote in towns.

County franchise: more restricted as farm labourers were seen as unfit to vote, but landowners and tenant farmers could vote.

Adullamites: led by Robert Lowe, they were opposed to any kind of democracy. John Bright gave them the name from the Cave of Adullam in the Old Testament where all the discontented had gathered.

Derby to be more active in resisting the reform. Buckle however believes Disraeli held back from attacks on Gladstone's Bill. Hoppen agrees that by letting the Adullamites do their work for them, Derby and Disraeli could sabotage vital parts of the proposals without seeming to be opposed to all reform. Hoppen believes Disraeli was especially effective in this way.

In June 1866, the Liberals resigned and Derby reluctantly agreed to undertake a third minority government. Disraeli again was Chancellor of the Exchequer. Ironically, it was Derby who suggested reform based on household suffrage. This would mean that all householders who paid their rates in person, rather than including rates in rent paid to the landlord, would qualify for the vote. There was also pressure from the Queen for reform and demonstrations in London urging reform. Historian Ian Machin argues that Derby and Disraeli were not spurred on to reform by riots in London as their progress on this subject was 'tentative and leisurely'. Machin considers that it was the minority position of the Conservatives and their need to improve their strength with a major piece of legislation, and also to maintain Liberal divisions which motivated them.

The Reform Bill

The details of the passing of the Reform Bill are fully outlined by both Lord Blake and John Walton. Lord Derby's first plan was to introduce 'a series of vague **Resolutions**' about some kind of reform. The Cabinet accepted this proposal and Disraeli suggested that reform be included in the Queen's Speech when Parliament was opened in February 1867. He envisaged the Resolutions, followed by a **Royal Commission** and then legislation in 1868.

It became clear to him that opinion in the House of Commons favoured more rapid action: Hoppen has pointed out how sensitive Disraeli was to **back-bench** opinion. However, some members of the Cabinet were reluctant to accept any moves towards household suffrage, so Disraeli's first proposals were modest (£6 **ratepayers** in towns and £20 tenants in counties). This failed to satisfy many Conservatives, so, as Terry Jenkins asserts, it was 'decided to sacrifice the three Cabinet ministers opposed to a more radical settlement; Lord Carnarvon, Lord Cranbourne and General Peel'. They duly resigned early in March.

The Conservatives now, as John Walton argues, favoured 'household suffrage with safeguards'. This was a popular slogan. The bill put forward in March 1867 gave the vote to personal ratepayers with two years residence with **plural voting** for the

Resolutions: Parliamentary proposals (but not in the form of legislation, and so simply an indication of future policy).

Royal Commission: a committee to investigate a problem or issue, often set up as a means of delaying any action.

Back-bench MPs: not members of the government, and often took an independent line and so needed to be placated by their leaders.

Ratepayers: paid local government taxes.

Plural voting: men owning property could vote in each constituency where they had property or land.

'The Derby 1867; Dizzy wins with "Reform Bill"'
A comment on Disraeli and the Reform Bill in *Punch* 1867.

Fancy franchises: a term describing a diverse series of proposed qualifications for the vote.

better off and '**fancy franchises**'. Gladstone opposed this but the Radicals were prepared to give it support and Disraeli needed their votes in order to build a majority in the House of Commons. He therefore accepted radical amendments while rejecting any proposed by Gladstone. As a result, the two year residential qualification was reduced to one year and lodgers in premises worth £12 a year were enfranchised. Most notably of all, Grosvenor Hodgkinson, MP for Newark, achieved temporary fame for his amendment abolishing **compounding** for rates so that all rates were to be paid in person and allowing an extra 0.5 million people to be enfranchised. The fancy franchises were ended, and in the counties, the voting qualification became £12 annual rent. John Stuart Mill proposed women should be given the vote on the same terms as men. This was defeated by 196 votes to 73 which Ian Machin describes as 'an encouragingly large majority'.

Compounding: the process where tenants paid rent (including their rates) to the landlord who then paid the local council. Other tenants and all house owners paid the council directly.

Disreali's power is strengthened

In August 1867, the Act became law and a Redistribution Act transferred a few seats from small boroughs to larger ones or to the counties, which was seen to favour the Conservatives. The UK electorate had doubled to nearly 2.5 million. Much of the credit for the Act went to Disraeli. John Walton feels this was 'emphatically Disraeli's measure' and 'went beyond anything Gladstone might have sanctioned'. Terry Jenkins agrees that Disraeli's 'personal reputation was considerably enhanced by the skill he displayed'. Hoppen considers Disraeli had succeeded in his aim 'to retain as best he could those aspects of the electoral system which had traditionally supported the Conservative Party'. Buckle points out that 'Every government of the last 15 years had taken the reform question in hand and every government had failed. Disraeli with a majority of 70 against him had carried his bill'. Thus his position in the Conservative Party was strengthened.

Maurice Cowling (*1867: Disraeli, Gladstone and Revolution,* 1967) emphasises this point and asserts that it was not only a victory over the Liberals but one within his own party which meant that 'Derby and Disraeli were going to run the Conservative Party, not Cranbourne and Peel'. It has been suggested that rivalry with Gladstone was a major motive for Disraeli. Buckle quotes a current joke:

Question: 'Why is Gladstone like a telescope?'

Answer: 'Because Disraeli draws him out, looks through him and shuts him up'.

Disraeli and Gladstone dressed in togas in a cartoon called 'The Two Augurs' which refers to the fact that Disraeli was the more successful party leader of the two.

But Sean Lang concludes that despite the undoubted personal animosity, Disraeli's prime aim was to get the bill passed. However, to combine this 'with the happy task of snubbing Gladstone at every opportunity was clearly welcome'.

After 1867, Disraeli claimed he had been 'educating his party' for years, certainly since 1859 to carry out his vision of democracy and asserted his belief in the good sense of the working man. He argued that reform was now shown to be no longer a Liberal monopoly, and the Conservatives now represented the whole nation. Terry Jenkins and John Walton both refute these claims which bore 'little relation to the truth of how and why the Reform Act was passed'. Walton points out that 'Disraeli himself had no idea of the electoral consequences of the Act' and the Conservative defeat in the 1868 Election would seem to support this conclusion. This defeat coming after Disraeli's brief period as Prime Minister seemed to leave him as far from permanent power as ever.

How did Disraeli become leader of the Conservative Party?

1. Read the following extract and answer the question.

> *'After complicated compromises, Disraeli was recognised by Stanley, in 1881, as the party leader in the Commons, though not enthusiastically. Disraeli soldiered on through long years on the opposition front bench. His attacks on Peel had brought him to the top of his weakened party, largely because almost all those ahead of him had followed Peel "into the wilderness". But he had the gift of seizing the unexpected opportunity and exploiting it. He also had the gift of patience; but the key event in his career was the 1867 Reform Act.'*

> (From Robert Blake, 'Disraeli: Political Outsider in Britain 1867–1918' in Catterall, P (ed.) *Britain 1867–1918*, Heinemann, 1955, pp. 57–8.)

Using this extract, assess how far Disraeli was lucky to become leader of the Conservative Party.

2. Robert Blake describes Disraeli as a 'political outsider'. Explain the seriousness of the obstacles which he had to overcome to become the Conservative leader.

2

Was Disraeli an opportunist in his foreign and imperial policies?

Was he committed to a more aggressive foreign and imperial policy before 1874?

Do events in South Africa and Afghanistan show he followed a 'forward' policy?

How far did his imperial policy continue that of the Liberals?

Did he have a consistent approach in his foreign policies and especially the Eastern Question?

Framework of events

1860–5	American Civil War between the North (anti-slavery and for the Union) and the South (pro-slavery and for Secession from the Union)
1865	Death of Palmerston
1868	Successful Abyssinian expedition
1870	Franco–Prussian War
1871	Establishment of the German Empire. Conference called by Gladstone over the Russian defiance of the Black Sea clauses
1872	Manchester and Crystal Palace speeches
1874	Ashanti war ended. New crown colony established in West Africa. Annexation of Fiji. Expedition to Perak
1875	Purchase of Suez Canal shares
1876	Royal Titles Act; Queen Victoria Empress of India. Gladstone's agitation about the 'Bulgarian Horrors'
1877–8	Russo–Turkish War
1878	British fleet to Constantinople. Russian invasion stopped short of Turkish capital. Treaty of San Stefano. Congress of Berlin and Treaty of Berlin
1878–9	Crisis in Afghanistan and South Africa

Imperialism: the attitudes of those who wanted to build up a powerful British Empire to enable Britain to maintain its prosperity and its major international role.

THE historian Paul Smith (*Disraeli, a Brief Life*, 1996) stated that Disraeli recognised, before many contemporaries, that **imperialism** could win his party votes. The historian Ian Machin (*Disraeli*, 1995) feels that Disraeli decided upon an imperialist foreign policy largely by chance, as the Manchester and Crystal Palace speeches did not deal in detail with imperial matters. Machin believes Disraeli 'took up and discarded policies' to maintain popularity and power.

Was Disraeli committed to a more aggressive foreign and imperial policy before 1874?

Historians such as John Walton (*Disraeli,* 1990) often quote two early examples to illustrate Disraeli's indifference to the colonies and hence his lack of commitment to expansion. In 1852, Disraeli wrote to a colleague 'These wretched colonies will all be independent in a few years and are a millstone round our necks'. In 1866, again referring to colonies 'which we do not govern' he categorised them as 'dead weights'. These comments were, however, largely aimed at the reluctance of Canada to pay for its own defence and are indicative of Disraeli's outlook as Chancellor of the Exchequer at the time.

Stembridge, in an article in the *Journal of British Studies* in 1965, pointed out that Disraeli's first political pamphlet, written in 1833, referred to his fears for the loss of 'our great Colonial Empire' and made it clear he wished to retain it. Moreover in his speeches in the 1830s and 1840s, Disraeli consistently favoured the maintaining of the authority of the mother country, that is Britain, over the Empire, although he accepted that 'colonies which govern themselves should defend themselves'. These were hardly examples of a new aggression but they do show a long term interest in colonial affairs.

Abyssinia: now Ethiopia, was an independent African kingdom.

British Consul: the Government's representative in Abyssinia.

The Abyssinian adventure

In 1866, when Disraeli was (for the third time) Chancellor of the Exchequer in a government headed by the fourteenth Earl of Derby, the **Abyssinian** adventure (1867–8) may have convinced him that there was political advantage to be gained from colonial issues. The Emperor Theodore of Abyssinia had taken the **British Consul** and other Europeans captive and a rescue mission was mounted in 1867. The Government feared a disastrous outcome: the death of captives and the failure of the expedition. In the event, Theodore was defeated and committed suicide, while the hostages were released in April 1868. The episode was brought to the attention of the British public through war correspondents such as **HM Stanley**.

The historian Muriel Chamberlain (*Pax Britannica? British Foreign Policy 1789–1914,* 1988) argues that the Government exploited the events in Abyssinia to take public attention away

HM Stanley (1841–1904)
Stanley was a war correspondent and also an explorer of the Congo in his own right. His best known exploit was to locate David Livingstone, the Scottish missionary searching for the source of the River Zambezi in 1871, and when successful to greet him with the words 'Dr Livingstone I presume'.

from emerging economic and social problems at home. Professor Freda Harcourt, in an article in the *Historical Journal* in 1980, argued this view more strongly, concluding that Disraeli deduced from these events that all classes could be brought together in support of a policy promoting national ideals. She also asserts that the intervention in Abyssinia was largely Disraeli's policy. On the other hand, historian Graham Goodlad (*British Foreign and Imperial Policy 1865–1919*, 2000) considers that it is not clearly evident that Disraeli played a large part in planning the expedition. He argues that the sole aim was to rescue the captives and to indicate to the ruler of Abyssinia his foolishness in arousing British anger. It was not an attempt to expand British influence. Once the captives were released, the British withdrew. There was no **annexation** of territory and so the episode hardly serves as an illustration of Disraeli's imperial ambition. To confirm this view, Ian Machin (*Disraeli*, 1995) suggests that it was an isolated episode which Disraeli may have seen as the first indication of what was later to be a central plank in his programme. It was, after all, similar to the kind of action taken by Palmerston in the past for which Disraeli had a good deal of admiration, even if Palmerston was a member of the opposing party.

Annexation: the taking over of colonial territories.

Manchester and Crystal Palace speeches

Further evidence for Disraeli's commitment to imperial issues comes from his **Manchester and Crystal Palace speeches** in 1872. It is clear that Disraeli's leadership of the Conservative Party was under threat at this point. A number of leading Conservatives met early in 1872 at Burghley House, the home of the Marquess of Exeter. It may be that some of them wished to replace Disraeli with Lord Derby or that their main aim was to encourage Disraeli into a more active role in opposition to the Liberal Government under Gladstone. Disraeli certainly began to show greater vigour both in and outside Parliament after this meeting.

The Manchester and Crystal Palace speeches: seen as central sources for the analysis of Disraeli's Conservatism where he supposedly redefined what the party stood for in a way that remained true well into the twentieth century.

North West Conservatives were treated to a lengthy address at the Free Trade Hall in Manchester in April 1872. In London in June, Disraeli gave a shorter but equally effective speech at the Crystal Palace. In these speeches, Disraeli blamed the Government for its failure to uphold Britain's interests overseas and developed the notion that all classes could be united by the imperial ideal. He argued that the working classes were enthusiastic about these themes. These speeches, Machin suggests, were responsible for boosting Conservative morale and Disraeli's own position as party leader. However, they did not indicate a distinctive Conservative commitment or policy. Eldridge (*Disraeli and the rise of a new Imperialism*, 1996) similarly sees the speeches in terms of party propaganda, repeating Disraeli's criticisms of the weak Liberal foreign policy. He also points out that the brief section on the empire in the Crystal Palace speech was largely ignored by the press at the time. Disraeli is again seen more as an opportunist than an architect of a new policy.

Disraeli took the opportunities given by Gladstone's first ministry to criticise his rival. He pointed to the cuts in defence expenditure, which he argued had reduced the effectiveness of the army and navy. He believed the balance of power in Europe had been destroyed by the Franco–Prussian War. The war also allowed Russia to cast aside the **Black Sea clauses** of the Treaty of Paris, 1856. He further blamed Gladstone for doing little and relying instead on international conferences. Over the ***Alabama* arbitration**, he was adamant that America was at fault with its '**rowdy rhetoric**'. This attitude often echoed public opinion. The historian, John Lowe, in *Britain and Foreign Affairs 1815–1885*, 1998, suggests that Disraeli showed more perception than Gladstone in this situation in that he was more aware of the significance of Prussia's defeat of France which the Liberals had accepted without taking any action. Disraeli also recognised the need to preserve prestige in Europe, for Britain to play a leading role and to show a degree of self-assertion in dealing with the Prussian Chancellor, Bismarck. Thus it can be argued that the foreign policies of the Liberals did have some effect on Disraeli's own ideas, but that his ideas were not yet part of a permanent policy.

Black Sea clauses: neither Russia nor Turkey was allowed to maintain a naval presence in the Mediterranean, thus preventing Russia from threatening British naval power.

***Alabama* arbitration**: Gladstone submitted the case for international arbitration which awarded the USA damages of £8.25 million and he duly paid up.

Rowdy rhetoric: this was how Disraeli described the outcry in America over the *Alabama* arbitration with which he did not sympathise.

How far did Disraeli's imperial policy continue that of the Liberals?

Forward imperial policy: the description of a policy based on advancing British frontiers and taking over more territories.

Defensible frontiers: natural boundaries such as mountain ranges, rivers and oceans.

John Lowe states conclusively that Disraeli did not set out to follow a '**forward**' **imperial policy**. He makes it equally clear that at first Disraeli followed the guidelines laid down by the preceding Liberal Government. This meant keeping the **defensible frontiers** already acquired in India and Asia. Eldridge supports this view. He emphasises the point that Disraeli, in 1874–5, inherited policies from the Liberals such as the annexation of Fiji and the increase in British influence in Perak, Malay. Proposals to annex other Pacific islands were rejected. On Disraeli's advice, a proclamation was issued in Perak specifically ruling out annexation. McIntyre (*The

Landmark Study   The book that changed people's views

Paul Smith, *Disraeli, a Brief Life* (Cambridge, 1996)

First published in 1996, Paul Smith makes use of the considerable recent reassessment of aspects of Disraeli's life and personality. His chief contribution is to discuss Disraeli's ideas and the influence his philosophy had on his political career. This is in contrast to the work of Lord Blake which concentrates on a political narrative. Smith is more concerned with Disraeli's 'intellectual and emotional' outlook. He argues that Disraeli did have a consistent outlook. He also argues that two essential Disraelian characteristics were his Jewishness and his romanticism. Both these influenced his imperialism. Smith stresses Disraeli's belief that preservation of the Empire would help to foster a sense of national purpose 'the duty which Providence has called upon us to fulfil'. Disraeli saw England as God's new chosen race. His romanticism enabled him to present a vision of Britain as 'more an Asiatic power than a European' with her Indian Empire and Turkey at the 'imperial centre of gravity'. Smith sees a strong anti-semitic element in the criticism of Disraeli's foreign and imperial policy, and a strong streak of romanticism in Disraeli at the Congress of Berlin, exercising the power for which he had striven for so long.

Imperial Frontier in the Tropics, 1865–75, 1967) agrees that Disraeli was far from initiating a forward policy and was content to follow policies worked out by the Liberals.

The foreign and imperial policy of Gladstone's First Ministry 1864–74

Gladstone's colonial secretary was Lord Kimberley who was reluctant to send troops to New Zealand to help the colonists against native Maoris. He made the South African province in the Cape of Good Hope self-governing in 1872, and he supported the Confederation of Canada giving Canada responsibility for its own defence. These were seen as examples of Liberal hostility to Empire.

Kimberley sent an expedition under Sir Garnet Wolseley, a capable soldier, to protect the Fante people of the West African Gold Coast (trading partners of the British) from attacks by the Ashanti, a rival tribe. He sent a new governor to Singapore who went on to appoint British 'residents' or advisors to the Malay states to extend British influence. He also sent Commander Goodenough to Fiji telling him to be cautious but Goodenough annexed the islands for Britain. These were seen as examples of a Liberal 'forward' policy and Disraeli continued what the Liberals had begun.

Do events in South Africa and Afghanistan show Disraeli followed a 'forward' policy?

Events in South Africa

Carnarvon (1831–90)
Carnarvon became colonial secretary in 1874 and was opposed to too much change. He lacked the ability to control the 'men on the spot' and resigned in 1878 when Disraeli seemed prepared to fight Russia in defence of Turkey. Disraeli nicknamed him 'Twitters' as he was so indecisive.

In South Africa, **Carnarvon** (Disraeli's colonial secretary) revived Kimberley's confederation scheme despite widespread opposition in the Cabinet, and when the **Boer** republics refused to cooperate, added the Transvaal to the Empire in 1877 without the Cabinet being consulted. Disraeli's role was to tell Carnarvon 'Do what you think wisest'. When the Boers remained discontented and Zulu unrest also surfaced, Disraeli blamed Carnarvon and wrote 'every day brings forward a new blunder of Twitters'. But the new colonial secretary, Hicks Beach, proved no more able to restrain the ambitions of Sir Bartle Frere and the disaster at Isandhlwana was the outcome. This was partly because the British forces were short of screwdrivers and could not open the boxes of ammunition fast enough. Disraeli felt he had to support his officials in public, while privately he suggested Frere 'ought to be impeached'. Disraeli can be blamed to some extent, but for a lack of supervision and at times lack of interest, rather than for a new aggressive policy. Historian, Edgar Feuchtwanger in *Disraeli*, 2000, agrees that in South Africa, Disraeli 'let things run' and was chiefly concerned to avoid trouble.

Boers: people of Dutch descent who had colonised in South Africa. They were often fervent Protestants.

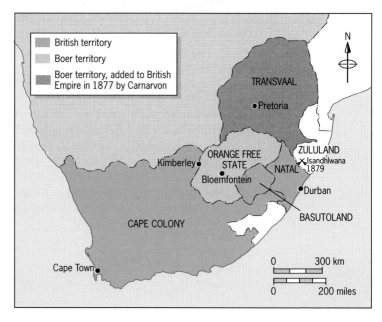

British territory
Boer territory
Boer territory, added to British Empire in 1877 by Carnarvon

TRANSVAAL
●Pretoria
Kimberley●   ORANGE FREE STATE   ZULULAND
Bloemfontein●   NATAL   ✕Isandhlwana 1879
●Durban
CAPE COLONY   BASUTOLAND
Cape Town●
0   300 km
0   200 miles
N

Southern Africa in 1877–9.

Events in Afghanistan

In Afghanistan, Disraeli had greater personal involvement. Historian John Lowe supports this view arguing that two of Disraeli's obsessions came together here, namely his desire to protect India, which had a special fascination for him, and his fear of Russia. His chief concern was to prevent Russia expanding into India and thus threatening the trade routes on which British power and prosperity depended. So when the Afghans accepted a Russian delegation in 1878, Lord Lytton, the Viceroy in India, took action and ordered a British Mission to enter Afghanistan. Lytton had been secretly instructed to persuade the Afghan ruler to accept a resident British representative and his appointment had been Disraeli's idea. Disraeli had deplored 'masterly inactivity' as a policy and expressed his support for Lytton. When Lytton exceeded his instructions and advanced on Kabul, Disraeli was appalled, but he defended Lytton in public.

The strategic location of Afghanistan in 1875.

Disraeli had not planned an Afghan war, but he had failed to control the man on the spot, and his reaction to events in Afghanistan shows his opportunism in reacting to success and failure. In addition, Eldridge and John Lowe agree that his policy was now perceived as imperialist and forward and his public speeches had encouraged this reaction. However, Maurice Cowling in the *English Historical Review* in 1961, ('Lytton, the Cabinet and the Russians, August to November, 1878') argued strongly that the war was very largely Lytton's fault.

Gladstone's criticism of Disraeli's policies

Midlothian campaigns: speeches made by Gladstone in Midlothian, Scotland, where he hoped to become the MP. He had retired as Liberal leader in 1875 but was making a comeback. He made over 30 speeches to over 85 000 people in total, and criticism of Beaconsfieldism was a key feature.

Beaconsfieldism: Gladstone's general term for the policies of Disraeli that he detested. In 1876, Disraeli had become Earl of Beaconsfield, the town nearest to his estate at Hughenden. His ennoblement was seen by some as a reward for making Queen Victoria Empress of India.

Interpretations of Disraeli's imperial policies have been inescapably influenced by the criticisms of Gladstone in his **Midlothian campaigns** in 1879 and 1880. Gladstone furiously condemned what he described as **Beaconsfieldism**, and in a famous passage, urged the electorate to 'remember the rights of the savage, remember that the sanctity of life in the hill villages of Afghanistan, among the winter snows, is as inviolable in the eyes of Almighty God as your own'. Gladstone further asserted that the wanton invasion of Afghanistan had 'made it a miserable ruin' while in Africa, the Government had annexed the Transvaal, an area inhabited by a free European, Christian, republican community.

Gladstone's motives for his accusations arose partly from his personal wish to return to the Liberal leadership. However, the effect was to establish Disraeli as an unprincipled, reckless warmonger with no regard for the twin pinnacles of Gladstonian Liberalism; moral principles and financial prudence. Modern historians such as John Walton and Eldridge have defended Disraeli, stating that he followed a coherent, premeditated policy of expansion.

Does the purchase of the Suez Canal shares show that Disraeli was an imperialist?

One instance over which historians unite is the purchase of the Suez Canal shares in November 1875. It is generally agreed by Smith, Machin, Feuchtwanger, Chamberlain and Eldridge that this was a personal initiative on Disraeli's part, which he had been considering for some time. The showmanship which he expressed over the issue in exaggerating the threat from the French and in his dramatic announcement to Queen Victoria 'It is just settled; you have it Madam', is equally typical of his ability to present his achievement to the public in the best possible light, despite the high

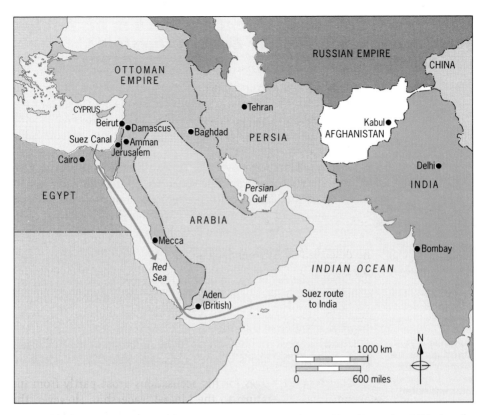

The Suez Canal and the Middle East in 1875 — the shortest route to India.

rate of interest, namely £100 000 charged by the Rothschilds for the four million pounds they advanced to the British Government. Historians are equally agreed that there was no real danger to the British use of the canal since freedom of passage was guaranteed by international agreement.

Marvin Swartz (*The Politics of British Foreign Policy in the era of Gladstone and Disraeli*, 1985) suggests that part of Disraeli's motivation lay in the need to fire the public imagination as his domestic reform programme was faltering by late 1875, but it is unlikely this was his prime aim. The need to be involved in the management of the canal, the shortest route to India, is consistent with Disraeli's view of the importance of India to Britain. In the winter of 1875–6, the Prince of Wales visited India, further evidence of Disraeli's view of its significance. Disraeli's Government remained extremely cautious over the possibility of more extensive intervention in Egypt and cooperated with the French in efforts to restore financial stability there, thus further suggesting that colonial expansion was not one of Disraeli's priorities in this instance.

Did Disraeli have a consistent approach in his foreign policies and especially the Eastern Question?

It is evident that Disraeli was eager to demonstrate that, unlike the previous Liberal Government, he intended to play a full part in foreign affairs. For Europe to act without her 'is not agreeable for a State like England' he wrote, while he told Queen Victoria in 1876 that 'consenting to play a secondary part does not become Your Majesty'.

Once problems arose over the Turkish Empire, Disraeli became fully involved, taking far more personal interest than he had shown in domestic reform. The so-called Eastern Question is a complex and difficult story, but there are some clear consistencies in Disraeli's actions. He followed traditional British foreign policy in his support for Turkey, regardless of moral issues, against encroaching Russia whom he saw as a threat to British India. This led him to agree to urge the Royal Titles Act on Parliament in 1876, making Victoria Empress of India and thus an equal of the **Tsar**. The main thrust behind this Act came from Queen Victoria, and Disraeli was unjustly blamed for imperial ambition in this respect.

Disraeli's apparent indifference to the sufferings of the **Bulgarian Christians** at the hands of the Turks, was strongly criticised by

Tsar: the ruler of Russia, at the time this was Alexander II.

Bulgarian Christians: lived under Turkish rule. They were members of the Orthodox Church while the Turks were Muslims and often mistreated their Christian subjects. The Turks had promised to amend their ways in the Treaty of Paris in 1856 and Britain hoped this would remove the Russian excuse for intervening in the Balkans, namely that they were protecting people of their own religion.

Disraeli dressed as Aladdin offering the crown of India to Queen Victoria. A cartoon in *Punch* in 1876.

**Marquess of Salisbury
(1830–1903)**
Salisbury was an aristocratic
senior member of the
Conservative Party and later
became Foreign Secretary in
Disraeli's Government and
later still, Prime Minister.

contemporaries. Gladstone is the best known of these. He exploded out of retirement with his pamphlet on the Bulgarian Horrors and the Question of the East in which he urged the Turks to leave Bulgaria 'bag and baggage'. Gladstone's solution to the problems in the Turkish Empire was for the Balkan countries to become independent nations. Disraeli had no time for the 'new-fangled, sentimental principle of nationality'.

Paul Smith argues that Disraeli was 'ready for any sacrifice of Turkish interests that British needs might require'. In this instance, Disraeli followed a consistent line. It was not a line which was always approved by his cabinet. His Foreign Secretary, Lord Derby, disliked any policy which might endanger peace, while Carnarvon and **Salisbury** both believed that some degree of self-rule should be granted to Balkan Christians, largely because of their own strong Christian beliefs. They also felt that Disraeli's policy was often short term, but Disraeli's biographers believe he showed great skill in a situation where Britain could only react to events and not shape them. John Lowe suggests Disraeli was left to 'cast around for a policy which would preserve the Sultan's independence', but agrees that support of Turkey was the mainstay of Disraeli's actions.

Support of Turkey, it seemed, might mean war with Russia. This was not Disraeli's aim, according to John Charmley (*Splendid Isolation? Britain and the Balance of Power 1874–1914*, 1999) who suggests he wanted to avert war 'by providing a "golden bridge" over which the Russians could retreat'. But in the Cabinet, Disraeli argued strongly that public opinion must be prepared for war and certainly Derby, his Foreign Secretary, believed that Disraeli was 'not drifting but rushing into war' in order to 'make foreign states think more highly of us'. Some members of the public urged Disraeli to act.

Plevna: a city attacked
by Russian troops led by
Todleben, an experienced
besieger. It held out for
five months to the surprise
of the Russians. By the
time Plevna fell, the British
had sent ships to defend
the Dardanelles which
commanded the naval
entrance to Constantinople.

Historian Paul Smith argues that, although Disraeli's efforts to influence the Russians by hinting that Britain might come to the aid of Turkey, failed to prevent Russia declaring war in 1877, the war itself helped his situation. The Turkish resistance at **Plevna** and the Russian advance on Constantinople signalled a patriotic outburst. Disraeli's secretary, **Montagu Corry**, reported to him

| **Montagu Corry 1840–1903** Corry became Disraeli's Private Secretary in 1866 and was devoted to him. | After Mary Anne died, he was indispensable and managed domestic matters. He was very loyal and kept Disraeli in touch with | gossip. When Disraeli died, his papers were left in Corry's safe hands. |

The Eastern Question

The Turkish Empire included the Balkans as well as Asia Minor and much of the Middle East. The Turks were Muslims but many of their subjects in the Balkans were Greek Orthodox Christians who were over-taxed and often ill-treated. The Turkish Empire was a barrier to Russian expansion into the Mediterranean and the Persian Gulf.

1875   The Christians began to revolt against Turkish rule in Bosnia and Herzegovina.

1876   Further uprisings in Greece and Bulgaria. The Berlin Memorandum was sent by nine European powers calling Turkey to make an armistice with the rebels. Disraeli was not part of this as he felt Britain had not been fully consulted. Britain sent their fleet to Besika Bay, which encouraged the Turks to reject the Memorandum. Stories that 25 000 Bulgarians had been massacred by the Turks reached London. Actual numbers were about 12 000. Gladstone published *The Bulgarian Horrors and the Question of the East* and sold 200,000 copies in a month. The Turks continued to advance in the Balkans and reject reforms, certain of British support.

1877   Russia declared war on Turkey in defence of the Christians and invaded Bulgaria. British public opinion now favoured the Turkish underdogs and feared the Russians would attack Constantinople.

1878   The Russians reached Adrianople. Disraeli's Cabinet agreed to intervene in favour of Turkey and send warships to defend Constantinople. Carnarvon resigned as colonial secretary in protest and later Derby also left the Government. Salisbury became Foreign Secretary. Russia forced the Treaty of San Stefano on Turkey with a much enlarged Bulgaria likely to come under Russian control and with a Mediterranean coast. Russia agreed to a conference to discuss these terms as Britain and Austria both protested. Salisbury's diplomacy secured a peaceful outcome. In June the Congress of Berlin took place in order to ratify the conventions already agreed: Romania and Serbia became independent, Bosnia and Herzegovina could be occupied by Austria–Hungary, Bulgaria became independent but much smaller, eastern Roumelia was given to Turkey with a Christian governor, Macedonia was returned to Turkey, Russia gained Batum as a port, Britain was given Cyprus in return for promises to protect Asian Turkey from Russia, and the Turks promised fair treatment of Christians.

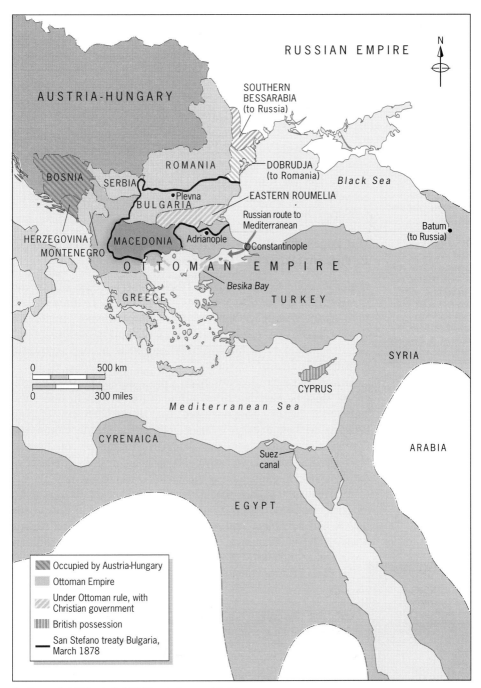

The Ottoman (Turkish) Empire in 1878 (after the Congress of Berlin).

'We don't want to fight but by Jingo! If we do
We've got the ships
We've got the men,
We've got the money too.
We've fought the bear before, and while we're Britons True.
The Russians shall not have Constantinople.'

The 'bear' is Russia. This chorus gave rise to the term 'Jingoism' to describe those eager for war to defend British Interests. Disraeli often called them the Jingoes.

Treaty of San Stefano: this was signed between Russia and Turkey in March 1878 and favoured Russia as she gained Bessarabia on the Black Sea. A large independent Bulgaria, known as 'Big Bulgaria' was set up with access to the Black Sea and the Aegean. Britain feared Russia would dominate Bulgaria and so gain access to the Mediterranean via the Aegean with no need to go through the Straits of the Dardanelles.

Holy Alliance: this refers to an alliance built up by Russia after 1815 with the other great powers which Britain had not joined.

on the **music-hall refrain** after a visit to the London Pavilion. The **Treaty of San Stefano** in 1878 and the establishment of the 'Big' Bulgaria, alarmed Austria and so made a European Conference a possibility.

Disraeli, as John Lowe asserts 'seized his chance' and ordered the fleet to defend Constantinople, called up reserves, asked Parliament for six million pounds and moved troops from India to Malta. Lord Salisbury replaced Lord Derby as Foreign Secretary and proved firmer and stronger than his predecessor. The resignation of Derby meant Disraeli's cabinet now became united behind his policy. In all its essentials, his policy remained the same.

Did Disraeli achieve his aims at the Congress of Berlin in 1878?

Historian John Charmley gives Disraeli every credit. 'It was the greatest moment of his career. He had set out to do three things: to break up what he thought was a new '**Holy Alliance**'; to prevent Russian expansion into Asia; and to raise the prestige and international standing of Britain; in all three areas he had enjoyed a considerable measure of success'.

Historian Edgar Feuchtwanger thinks Salisbury deserves the credit, since he negotiated the outline of the settlement before the conference began. This included the dismemberment of 'Big Bulgaria' to keep Russian influence out of the Mediterranean, the Cyprus Convention and the Austrian occupation of Bosnia-Herzegovina. John Lowe attributes a good deal to 'Bismarck's ruthless chairmanship, forcing the weaker states to give way'.

All historians agree that Disraeli sparkled at Berlin in an amazing personal triumph. The world he had depicted in his novels had become a reality. There was a huge demand for his books in Berlin. **Bismarck**, whom Disraeli had last met in 1862, by the end of the conference declared 'The old Jew, he's the man'. The two of them enjoyed long sessions together, respecting one

Bismarck (1815–98)
Otto von Bismarck was a Prussian landowner who became Chief Minister in 1862. His policy of 'blood and iron' using war to get

his way was extremely successful, leading to the defeat of France in 1871 and the creation of the German Empire under Kaiser Wilhelm I with

Bismarck as his Chancellor. He acted as Chairman at Berlin.

Real politik: policies based on realities, especially material needs rather than ideals or moral principles.

another as practitioners of **real politik**. Disraeli was an amazing social success and feted at dinner parties, one of his favourite stages on which to perform. He was dissuaded from making his main speech in French by the claim that the diplomats were eager to hear 'the greatest living master of English oratory' in his own language. In fact, Disraeli's French was so bad that few could understand it.

Peace with honour

When Disraeli and Salisbury returned to Britain, they claimed to be bringing 'peace with honour'. Queen Victoria was certainly eager to load him with honours, but Disraeli refused a Dukedom, accepting only the **Garter** and insisting that Salisbury should also receive it. Terry Jenkins (*Disraeli and Victorian Conservatism*, 1996) calls the Congress of Berlin, Disraeli's 'finest hour' and adds that the crisis had allowed Disraeli to rally his party behind him while the Liberals were divided, with **Hartington** largely with Disraeli and Gladstone firmly opposed.

Garter: the Order of the Garter, England's first order of chivalry and the personal gift of the monarch.

Lord Hartington (1833–1908)
Hartington later became the eighth Duke of Devonshire and led the Liberals after Gladstone retired in 1875. He disliked Gladstone's excitability over Bulgaria but, in 1880, soon saw that Gladstone, after the Liberal victory, was bound to become Prime Minister again. He was seen as the last of the leading Whigs. He was a conscientious but uninspired leader and made it easy for Disraeli to dominate in the House of Commons. Disraeli usually referred to him as 'Harty-Tarty'.

Crowds at Charing Cross on Disraeli's return from Berlin in 1878 congratulating him on the gains he had made for Britain

Favourable assessments of what was achieved at Berlin include Paul Smith's belief that Disraeli had been able to 'secure a leading role in a European settlement which preserved what he had defined as essential British interests and provided **Cyprus** as a further bastion of their defence … He had made Britain count'.

Cyprus: a Mediterranean island and part of the Turkish Empire. It was ceded to Britain in the Cyprus Convention of 1878 as payment for Britain's help in the defence of Turkey from Russia. Disraeli hoped it would be a more useful naval base than Malta as it was closer to the Suez Canal.

Lord Blake considers that although the Berlin Settlement had its faults, 'it was followed by a long period of peace between the European powers'. Historian Richard Shannon (*The Crisis of Imperialism, 1865–1915*, 1976) takes the opposite view that Disraeli achieved very little as most of the settlement was rapidly undone. Ian Machin's judgement is also more reserved. He recognises that the defence of Turkey, so vital to India, had 'been clearly attained', but he too suggests that the Bulgarian settlement was short lived and even Cyprus did not have permanent significance as a naval base.

Contemporaries were not necessarily impressed by Disraeli's achievements. His brinkmanship over the possibility of war with Russia was seen as dangerous, and his movement of Indian troops without Parliamentary sanction was seen as a disregard of constitutional safeguards. Equally, the occupation of Cyprus was agreed without the knowledge of Parliament. Some even accused Disraeli of **Caesarism**, aiming at a military dictatorship on the Roman model. Derby considered Disraeli was at fault for making his policy dependent on public opinion which was notoriously fickle; vehemently against the Turks in 1876 and all for them 18 months later. Gladstone of course, was outraged. He saw no honour in acquiring possessions like Cyprus, where Britain would remain a foreign master. Disraeli was guilty of 'territorial aggrandisement backed by military display'. Disraeli, in response, claimed Gladstone was 'a sophistical rhetorician inebriated by the exuberance of his own verbosity', that is to say drunk with words.

Caesarism: one of the accusations made by Disraeli's enemies that in his foreign and imperial policies, he acted as a dictator like a Roman Emperor, without any regard for Parliament.

Long term results of the Berlin Settlement

The long term results tend to support Salisbury's view that protecting Turkey in Europe was a lost cause.

- The rift between Austria and Russia did not last and by 1881 another League was formed again isolating Britain.

- In 1885, the division of Bulgaria ended when it absorbed eastern Roumelia, leading Bulgaria to look to Austria and Germany for protection against Russia.

- Turkish promises of reform came to nothing.

- Austrian occupation of Bosnia and Herzegovina led to Slav unrest in the Balkans and to Russian support of Slavs in Serbia contributing to the First World War.

- The Turkish Sultan came to resent the loss of Cyprus and the guarantee to Turkey in Asia proved difficult in practice.

- Balkan peoples remained under Turkish rule and were resentful, so the Eastern Question was not resolved.

- The return of Macedonia to Turkey was the cause of the First Balkan War in 1912 which led to the First World War as the Balkan troubles increased the inter-power rivalries of Europe.

- Gladstone's support for independent Balkan states in the long term was not only morally preferable but also politically sound.

Was Disraeli's Eastern policy consistent?

1. Read the following extract and answer the question.

   'Lord B (Disraeli as the Earl of Beaconsfield) is determined that the Russians shall not directly or indirectly become possessed of Constantinople. He said it was obvious that if the Russians had Constantinople, they could at any time march their army through Syria to the mouth of the Nile and then what would be the use of our holding Egypt? Not even the command of the sea could help us under such circumstances.'

   (A memorandum by Lord Barrington after a conversation with Disraeli. From W.L. Monypenny and G.E. Buckle *Life of Benjamin Disraeli* volume II, John Murray, 1929, p 956.)

   Using this extract and your own knowledge, consider how far Disraeli's policy on the Eastern Question centred on his fear of Russia.

2. How justified is the view that Disraeli achieved little lasting security for Britain in his policy on the Eastern Question?

> *Is there evidence of an interest in social reform before 1868?*

> *Was a vote-winning programme of social reform outlined in his 1872 speeches?*

> *Did his Second Ministry show he was a genuine social reformer?*

Framework of events

1844–7	Publication of *Coningsby*, *Sybil*, and *Tancred*, a trilogy of novels investigating the political, social and spiritual condition of England
1867	Second Reform bill, seen by Disraeli as the logical outcome of the ideas in the novels
1866–8	Conservative ministry passed social reforms to improve working-class housing, extend the Factory Acts and remedy the poor health of London paupers, hoping to appeal to new voters
1872	Disraeli's speeches at Manchester and Crystal Palace, London, favouring sanitary reform and improvements in working hours and conditions to 'elevate the condition of the people'
1874–6	As Prime Minister, Disraeli oversaw a range of social reform measures
1877–80	Fewer social reforms passed as foreign affairs took priority and as economic recession, notably in farming, meant expenditure needed to be reduced

Is there evidence of an interest in social reform before 1868?

In the 1840s, Disraeli and the Young England Group had criticised the **Poor Law** and supported the **Ten Hours Movement**. Terry Jenkins argues that the young noblemen in the group had made their judgements uninfluenced by Disraeli, but that his contribution came

Poor Law: this was established in 1834 to force the poor into unpleasant workhouses in order to get any assistance. Its aim was to save money on the local rates by cutting poor relief, since the poor would only enter a workhouse as a last resort.

Ten Hours Movement: this was a prolonged campaign to limit normal working hours in factories for women and children to ten hours a day. This was achieved in 1847, but in 1850, women and children's hours were limited to between 6.00am and 6.00pm with an hour for meals and 6.00am to 2.00pm on Saturdays. This effectively increased their hours to 10.5 hours a day.

Condition of England: this reflected concern for social conditions, especially in industrial towns, and resulted in unrest.

Public Health bills: these established a Central Board of Health and local boards but were unpopular for enforcing expensive measures to stop the spread of diseases like cholera. They were also seen as an interference with individual freedom.

Trade unions: established in the 1850s, these were largely for skilled workers and preferred bargaining to striking for their aims.

Peaceful picketing: trying to persuade workers to join a strike, not by intimidating them but by peaceful means.

One Nation Toryism: stresses the need to improve the conditions of people as a whole and so prevent the emergence of a divided society. Disraeli is credited with the idea after his description of the Two Nations (the rich and the poor) in *Sybil*.

from his novels. The '**Condition of England**' was a fashionable topic for debate and in *Sybil* (published in 1945), Disraeli outlined the evils of factory labour and what Paul Smith described as 'a cleavage' between the 'two nations of rich and poor' to be resolved by 'equality not by levelling the Few but by elevating the Many'. John Vincent (*Disraeli*, 1990) considers that in the Young England novels (*Coningsby*, *Sybil* and *Tancred*) Disraeli put forward general proposals for social harmony such as gentry rule and peace between the classes 'merging into mutual affection'. Vincent does not see social compassion or anger in the books but detachment and above all, irony.

Disraeli helped to ensure the passing of the Ten Hours bill in 1847 and was against its amendment in 1850. On the other hand, as Paul Smith points out, Disraeli opposed an Inspection of Mines bill 'to please his coal-owning friend Lord Londonderry' and was against the **Public Health bills** in 1848 and 1854, because they gave too much power to central government. In the 1850s when in office, he showed some readiness to talk to **trade-unionists** about **peaceful picketing** but did not 'lay the basics of a combination between Toryism and the working classes'. The conclusion to be drawn from this is that before 1868, Disraeli cannot be described as committed to social reform.

One nation

The '**One Nation**' ideal has also been associated with Disraeli in this period. In a speech in 1862 he outlined Tory policy: 'to favour popular education because it is the best guarantee of public order, to defend local government and to be as jealous of the rights of the working man as of the prerogative of the Crown'. In 1867 he claimed the Reform Act had 'taken a happy opportunity to enlarge the privileges of the people of England. We have not done anything but strengthen the institutions of the country, the essence of whose force is that they represent the interests and guard the rights of the people'. Again this indicates that Disraeli's contribution was based more on presentation than in reality. It was convenient, and one of his constant concerns, to present the Conservative Party as uniting the classes, but this did not mean it did so.

Disraeli introduces the Reform Bill in 1867 which would add more than one million voters to the electorate.

Was a vote-winning programme of social reform outlined in Disraeli's 1872 speeches?

In his speeches at Manchester and Crystal Palace, Disraeli attacked Gladstone's Government and indicated his own Tory principles. Little was new in his assertion of the virtues of the monarchy, the House of Lords and the Church of England. It was, however, possible to argue that these institutions were to an extent threatened by the Liberals and this gave a new urgency to his views. Jenkins argues that in stressing that 'Conservative' applied to the 'people of England and especially the working classes of England' who 'are proud of belonging to a great country and wish to maintain its greatness' Disraeli had in mind '**Tory democracy**' although he did not use the actual term.

Feuchtwanger points out that the references to social reform were quite short and lacking in detail. Disraeli did mention housing, air, light and water, factory inspection and purity of food, although not with any kind of detailed plans for reform. These were problems which had been discussed for a long time and, says Feuchtwanger, 'Disraeli had concerned himself with them at least since the publication of *Sybil*'.

There was little here that could be described as a programme. It was only in retrospect that the speeches were seen as guidelines to the future. In any case, Disraeli had attacked Gladstone for harassing every interest and class with too much legislation and had made his famous comparison of Gladstone and his ministers with 'a range of exhausted volcanoes' so it was unlikely he would wish to do likewise.

Tory democracy: a term first used by Lord Randolph Churchill in the 1880s, but seen as defining Disraeli's new Conservatism and his belief that the long established institutions should use their power wisely for the good of all and especially to help working people. It has been suggested Disraeli wanted to win votes from the workers and this was his main motive in social reform.

Conservative victory in 1874

As for the 1874 victory, it was arguably more a fact that the Liberals were defeated than the Conservatives were victorious. Jenkins argues that the Conservative victory in 1874 was the result of increasing middle class support. The middle classes had expanded to include tradesmen and white collar workers as well as the rich trading class, and to such groups Disraeli's speeches had undoubted appeal, despite their lack of detailed proposals. Yet it must also be admitted that personally, Disraeli did little to reconcile the class divides. His Cabinet in 1874 was largely aristocratic, apart from Richard Cross and W.H. Smith 'the bookstall man'. Derby noted his 'odd dislike of middle-class men, though they are the strength of our party'.

As for the working class, John Walton shows how Disraeli resisted the formation of working-class Conservative Clubs which

John Gorst (1835–1916)
Gorst was asked by Disraeli in 1868 to improve Party organisation. He was highly efficient and ensured the large boroughs with new working class voters had good Tory candidates. He coordinated Party activities throughout the country and drew on the unoccupied middle-class women to help distribute propaganda. He was credited with the 1874 Conservative victory. He became an MP in 1875 but was very quarrelsome and cantankerous and his organisation became less effective.

ran counter to his portrayal of the Tory Party as a national party for all classes. He insisted that these clubs be controlled by constituency organisations run by men of property, appointing **John Gorst** as the central Party organiser in 1870. Walton concludes that this was not a sustained 'commitment to practical Tory democracy such as the Disraeli legend might lead us to expect'.

Did Disraeli's Second Ministry show he was a genuine social reformer?

Lord Blake described the measures shown in the box opposite as 'impressive' and 'taken together they constitute the biggest instalment of social reform passed by any one government in the nineteenth century'. But Blake, like other historians writing on this topic, makes it clear that he does not see this as an aristocratic alliance with the 'working masses', so denying One Nation Toryism was at work here. Nor does he see the measures as a 'substantial shift from *laissez-faire* to state intervention'. They were generally cautions and permissive, far from producing any kind of welfare state. Disraeli had asserted '**Permissive legislation** is the characteristic of a free people'. There were also constraints in that tax payers and rate payers were no more willing, then than now, to meet excessive demands and the 1874 Budget reduced income tax and some indirect taxes.

John Walton considers that the social reforms were not a Disraelian programme but a series of responses to problems. The new Government had campaigned against the disruption of the Liberals, so was hardly likely to embark on a frenzy of legislation itself. Walton argues that the measures had varying origins. Some such as the Friendly Societies Act, the Merchant Shipping Act, the Public Health Act and the Rivers Pollution Act arose from Royal Commissions set up by the previous Liberal Government. Some came from pressure groups, including the Lancashire Conservative

Laissez-faire: a French phrase meaning 'leave it alone'. A belief that government should interfere in the lives of people as little as possible and let economic forces take their course.

Permissive legislation: where the observance of a law is not compulsory but it can be applied, often by a local authority.

Landmark Study The book that changed people's views

Robert (Later Lord) Blake, *Disraeli* (Methuen, 1966)

Blake aimed to make a fresh appraisal of Disraeli's career with the emphasis on politics which he saw as the 'breath of Disraeli's life'. It has been described as 'one of the very few great political biographies' and still holds sway as the major source for all students of Disraeli. Blake gives special praise to Disraeli's social measures which he sees as a great reforming programme. He used a wider range of sources than Monypenny and Buckle and presents a more rounded and less flattering view of Disraeli. Blake's narrative strength seems unlikely to be surpassed but he is less convincing in his analysis of Disraeli's intellectual and emotional development according to Paul Smith, and tends to 'push Disraeli's ideas to the periphery' (edge) while defending him from the usual charges of 'insincerity and lack of principle'.

Samuel Plimsoll (1824–98)
Plimsoll was the radical Liberal MP for Derby who worked to save the lives of seamen in overloaded ships. When the Act was delayed he lost his temper in the house and shouted 'villains' at the Conservatives. It was 1890 before the Act was really effective. He is commemorated by the Plimsoll line which shows the level to which a ship may be safely loaded.

MPs who had campaigned for a nine hour day, and the brewers who wanted revision of the unpopular 1872 Licensing Act. **Samuel Plimsoll** argued strongly for a loading line for merchant shipping to outlaw 'coffin ships' and went so far as to shake his fist at Disraeli when the bill stalled in the House of Commons, largely as a result of the incompetence of Sir Charles Adderley, the responsible minister.

Many of the bills were the initiative of active individual ministers. **Richard Cross**, the Home Secretary, was surprised to find Disraeli's mind was not 'full of legislative schemes' and 'he had to rely entirely on the various suggestions of his colleagues'. Cross responded nobly with the Licensing Act, the Artisans Dwelling Act and two Factory Acts. Lord Sandon introduced the Education Act, and Sclater-Booth, the President of the Local Government Board, the Public Health Act.

The Torrens Act of 1868, blocked by House of Lords, would have covered similar ground to the Artisan's Dwelling Act. Colin Matthew, in his edition of Gladstone's Diaries (1982) makes it clear that the Liberals were preparing trade union legislation similar to that of the Conservatives. Factory and public reforms had cross-party support. Robert Lowe, a prominent Liberal was a vocal supporter of the peaceful picketing clauses in the Conspiracy and Protection of Property Act. Samuel Plimsoll combined with Tory MPs for constituencies containing ports to press for the Merchant Shipping Act.

Richard Cross (1823–1914)
Cross was a successful lawyer and businessman from Lancashire. He was the least experienced member of the Cabinet and was appointed in recognition of the part played by Lancashire in the Conservative victory. He was hard working and perceptive and one of the real successes of the Government.

Can Disraeli be credited with the reforms?

Two questions remain about the reforms. One relates to how much credit can be given to Disraeli and the other to how far reaching the reforms were. Again, the historians are largely agreed. Lord Blake concludes 'it would be wrong to pitch Disraeli's claims too high as author of this valuable legislation'. Feuchtwanger argues that Disraeli interfered little with department ministers, which made for a harmonious atmosphere, 'except when he sensed a political issue'. As an example, in 1875 he insisted on a reduction of income tax by 1d, the ending of the sugar duty and the allocation of £1.25 million from central government for lunatic asylums and the police, to ease the burden on ratepayers and thus keep their support. This allowed Disraeli to counter Gladstone's pledge to abolish income tax and to maintain the balance between direct and indirect taxation.

Jenkins agrees that Disraeli was not very active in social reform and even fell asleep in cabinet discussions leading Derby to write 'The work is too heavy for a man over 70'. Jenkins argues that Disraeli's approach was cautious despite his assertions about the 'condition of the people', but that he remained 'faithful to his stated view that useful, non-contentious social reform measures were an appropriate form of action for the Conservatives'. Angus Hawkins (*British Party Politics 1852–86*, 1998) likewise sees Disraeli's interest in the details as slight and argues 'his great achievement was to provide a rhetorical context for the Acts' and 'to place the social condition of the people near the top of the political agenda'. Both Jenkins and Hawkins also agree that Disraeli wished to draw a contrast with the 'overbearing restlessness' of the Liberals with their attacks on the privileges of the church and aristocracy.

Lord Blake considers Disraeli did take an interest in the trade union question and in the Agricultural Holdings Act, but could equally be vague. For example, Disraeli wrote in 1874 'I believe that **Mr Secy X** is working on a Dwellings bill', although later he asserted that the Act was in 1875 'our chief measure'. For some of the 1874–6 period, Disraeli was often ill and criticised as 'incompetent' by some MPs. Disraeli recognised he was becoming less effective in the House of Commons and so, rather than resign, accepted a peerage in 1876.

Mr Secy X: this was how Disraeli referred to Cross, the Home Secretary.

Were the reforms effective and far reaching?

As for the effectiveness of the reforms, there is again little real disagreement among the main writers on the period. Ian Machin's judgement is that 'the large cluster of social Acts did not produce any collective revolutionary change and was not intended to do so'. He cites the Artisan's Dwelling Act as permissive legislation taken up by only ten of the 87 towns to which it applied up to 1881. The Friendly Societies Act was also a 'rather minimal effort'. John Walton adds that the River Pollution measure failed 'to define pollution or to provide ways of punishing the polluters' while the Sale of Food legislation failed 'to compel local authorities to employ analysts'. Florence Nightingale was perhaps optimistic in claiming 'poor baby will have a better chance of getting beyond babyhood now'. Some of these failings came about because of the reluctance of Sir Stafford Northcote, the Chancellor of the Exchequer, to spend money.

Some Acts were more definite in dealing with particular issues and the interests of particular groups. The Intoxicating Liquor Act extended licensing hours in the interests of brewers and publicans. The Factory Act reduced the working hours for women and children to meet the demands of the nine hour movement and, incidentally, by introducing the half day on Saturday, enabled the Football League to prosper. The Education Act did enforce school attendance in rural areas, and children aged 10–14 could not be employed without a certificate of school attendance or academic attainment. Many back-bench MPs felt that too much education for rural children might lead them to be critical of the **status quo**. The Public Health Act was compulsory, gathering many earlier provisions into one statute and did, says Jenkins, 'provide a durable settlement for this area of policy'.

Status quo: a Latin phrase meaning unchanged situation.

The most important area of reform with a 'wider political significance', according to Jenkins, lay in the trade union laws. Richard Cross decided to advance from a Royal Commission report to meet the demands of the **Trade Union Congress (TUC)**. Here Cross argued he was 'putting workmen on an equal legal footing with their employer' which he felt was consistent with the principles of the day. Walton considers these were the only 'straight-forwardly successful' of the reforms which settled the issue for a generation. Lord Blake agrees that these were 'much the most successful of the Conservative social reforms'. Disraeli did give these reforms his backing in a hostile Cabinet. He later claimed, 'We have settled the long and vexatious contest between capital and labour' and, significantly but improbably, he hoped to 'gain and retain for the Tories the lasting affection of the working class'.

Trade Union Congress (TUC): set up in 1868 by several unions to represent them. They were eager to secure a legal basis for unions and also to make strikes legal.

The programme of reform was in any case, quite short lived. By 1876, a real political issue had arisen in Bulgaria and apart from a Factory Act in 1878, little further social reform emerged. Ghosh, in

Social reform 1874–8

1874 Factory Act
- Maximum hours for women and children to be 56.5 per week.
- Children under 10 not to be employed.
- No full time work until a child was 14.

1874 Intoxicating Liquors Act
- Opening hours extended by 30 minutes.
- Clauses from 1872 Act to stop watering of beer were removed.
- Fewer police rights to enter pubs.
- Brewers and publicans rewarded for their support in the election.

1875 Public Health Act
- Local authorities to provide adequate drainage, water supply and sewage disposal.
- Offensive items in streets were to be removed.
- Markets, street lighting and burials were regulated.
- Infectious diseases were to be notified.

1875 Artisans' Dwelling Act
- Influenced by the Cholera outbreak of 1866–7.
- Local authorities could buy slums and rebuild with more sanitary houses.
- No compulsion and generally ignored.
- Used by Joseph Chamberlain, the Mayor of Birmingham to some effect.

1875 Sale of Food and Drugs Act
- Established rules for preparation of food for sale.
- Set up inspectors to detect adulterated food, e.g. chalk in flour.
- No compulsion for local authorities to appoint inspectors so not effective.

1875 Conspiracy and Protection of Property Act
- Liberal Act of 1871 had been very unpopular.
- Peaceful picketing became legal.
- Unions could act legally as a group and so could strike.

1875 Employers and Workman Act
- Replaced Master and Servant Act with more equal terms.
- Both employers and workmen were on equal footing in cases of breach of contract.
- It became a civil offence in both cases to break contracts

1875 Friendly Societies Act
- Societies provided insurance for the working classes.
- Royal Commission set up as there were fears they were financially unsound.
- Societies were to register voluntarily.
- Tables of model premiums drawn up but were permissive.
- Infants could still be insured but for limited amounts.

1875 Agricultural Holdings Act
- Aimed to secure the position of tenant farmers.
- Permissive; landlords and tenants could adopt it if they wished. Not very effective.

1876 Enclosures Act
- Common land to be preserved for public use. Led to the 'greenbelt'.
- Epping Forest safeguarded for Londoners' recreation in 1878 as a result.

1876 River Pollution Act
- Based on a Royal Commission.
- Noxious substances not to be dumped in rivers.
- Prosecution needed Local Government Board permission so rarely happened.

1876 Education Act
- Local School Attendance Committees to make attendance compulsory.
- Children under 10 not to be employed.
- Children aged 10–14 could work part time if they had a certificate of attendance or of academic attainment.
- Aim was to help Anglican schools in competition with rate-funded board schools.
- Unnecessary school boards could be dissolved.

1876 Merchant Shipping Act
- Stop-gap measure passed in 1875.
- Pressure from Samuel Plimsoll and Tory MPs for ports to stop overloading ships.
- Plimsoll line to be painted on ships to show the maximum loading point. In reality painted on ships wherever owner wanted, so did little to ensure safety of sailors.

1878 Factory and Workshop Act
- Local authorities to inspect workshops employing fewer than 50 people.

Before (top) and after (bottom) the reforms in Birmingham. Slums were pulled down and Corporation St was built.

an essay in Waller (ed.) *Politics and Social Change in Modern Britain* (1987), argues that Disraeli was planning more measures for 1880 until he lost the election, but he does admit 1877–9 was a 'legislative desert'. There was a failed effort in 1879 to disband the eight private water companies supplying water to London.

Bruce Coleman (*Conservatism and the Conservative Party in Nineteenth Century Britain*, 1988) adds another perspective to the assessment. He points out that back-bench Conservatives would not take kindly to higher taxes resulting from reforms, or to measures which increased state responsibility for individuals and worked against the interests of property owners, the backbone of the party. So even limited reforms, notably in education and agriculture, met resistance. The working class were vociferous in their demand for trade union reform and strong supporters of Plimsoll and the merchant sailors betrayed by greedy immoral ship owners, but otherwise they were not particularly eager to reform either.

In view of these provisos, John Walton concludes that Disraeli 'may not have lived up to the expectations that are aroused by the legend and the myth' but 'in the context of his time and the ideas he made a difference to the Party's programme as well as to its image'. He goes on 'The social reform programme of 1874–6 was a sustained gesture' to a harmonious society 'and Disraeli promised it, publicised it, took ostentatious pride in it and allocated time to it. It is all very well and salutary to emphasise what Disraeli did not do, but what he did do was very important indeed, and it even made a difference, however small, to the living conditions of some of those at whom the legislation was directed'. One of Disraeli's back-benchers made a shorter but equally valid assessment. It was 'suet-pudding legislation; it was flat, insipid, dull, but it was very wise and very wholesome'.

Were Disraeli's social reforms a result of a new Conservative philosophy?

1. Read the following extract and answer the question.

   '*It is an exaggeration to regard them [the social reforms] as the product of a fundamentally different political philosophy from that of the Liberals, or to see in them the fulfilment of some concept of the paternalistic Tory democracy which had been proposed by Disraeli in opposition to Peel during the 1840s and now at last had reached fruition*'.

   (From Robert Blake, *Disraeli*, Methuen, 1966, p 553.)

   Using this extract and your own knowledge, consider how far Disraeli's social reforms represented a new Tory policy.

2. How justified is the view that Disraeli had little personal enthusiasm or interest in social reforms?

Disraeli: an assessment

Disraeli and the Conservative Party

Disraeli made the Conservative Party electable again after years in opposition as a result of the 1846 split. He helped to improve its administration, setting up the Central Office. He gave it some of its core beliefs in the Crown, the Church and the Empire as well as making it the party that had an appeal to all classes and thus expressed national unity.

Imperial and foreign affairs

In many ways, Disraeli's preservation of British interests reflected the same priorities as those of the Liberal Party. His contribution lay in presenting issues in 'Jingoistic' terms and in his own special achievements like the Suez Canal Shares and the acquisition of Cyprus.

Social reform

Here Disraeli showed a cautious approach to State intervention. He tried to reassure the propertied classes that the Conservatives would govern responsibly while gaining support from the working classes with his measures to improve their living and working conditions.

Disraeli's legacy

In Conservative Party circles, Disraeli has always been a great hero; the man who inspired the working classes with a love for the country's great institutions. He was credited with the ideas of Tory democracy and One Nation politics and both slogans were taken up by later Conservatives, including Joseph Chamberlain the former Liberal who, in the 1890s, claimed that the introduction of old age pensions would be in the Disraeli tradition. Even in the 1920s, his devotion to social reform was being rekindled as the Conservatives tried to meet the challenges of the Labour Party.

After his death, the Primrose League was founded in 1883 to perpetuate his ideals and on Primrose Day, April 19, the anniversary of his death, his memory was celebrated. The League was instrumental in bringing the working classes into the party and, like Disraeli, especially appealed to women. More recently, Disraeli has been admired for his flexibility and his readiness to accept anything that would help his party to power. His persistence and determination in the face of setbacks appeal to the champions of the underdog, while some aspects of his career throw light on anti-semitism in Victorian England.

Further reading

Texts specifically designed for students

Goodlad, G.B. *British Foreign and Imperial Policy 1865–1919* (Routledge, 2000)

Jenkins, T.A. *Disraeli and Victorian Conservatism* (Macmillan, 1996)

Walton, J.K. *Disraeli* (Routledge, 1990)

Texts for more advanced study

Blake, R. *Disraeli* (Methuen, 1966) is the standard political biography, heavily based on the detailed work of W.F. Monypenny and G.E. Buckle written in 1910–20.

Eldridge, C.C. *Disraeli and the Rise of a New Imperialism* (University of Wales Press, 1996) considers that Disraeli consistently argued for the power, status and prestige of the British Empire.

Feuchtwanger, E. *Disraeli* (Arnold, 2000) emphasises Disraeli's iconic status as well as his triumph as an outsider.

Machin, I. *Disraeli* (Longman, 1995) is a more critical view considering that Disraeli's quest for power mattered more to him than consistent policies.

Smith, P. *Disraeli, a Brief Life* (Cambridge, 1996) takes a fresh look at Disraeli's ideas and his unique character.

Vincent, J. *Disraeli* (Oxford, 1990) is a very lively account of Disraeli's views on race, religion and politics largely based on a detailed examination of his novels.

Walton, J.K. *The Second Reform Act* (Methuen, 1983) sees Disraeli as mainly opportunist in passing the Act.

Index

Published by HarperCollins*Publishers* Ltd
77–85 Fulham Palace Road
London
W6 8JB

Browse the complete Collins catalogue at
www.collinseducation.com

© HarperCollins*Publishers* Ltd 2004
First published 2004

ISBN 0 00 717322 9

British Library Cataloguing in Publication Data. A catalogue record for this book is available from the British Library.

Series commissioned by Graham Bradbury
Project management by Will Chuter
Edited by Rebecca Harman
Book and cover design by Derek Lee
Map artwork by Richard Morris
Picture research by Celia Dearing
Production by Sarah Robinson
Printed and bound by Martins, Berwick upon Tweed

ACKNOWLEDGEMENTS

The Publishers would like to thank the following for permission to reproduce extracts from their books:

John Murray for an extract from *Life of Benjamin Disraeli Volume II*, by W. L. Monypenny and G. E. Buckle (1929).

The Publishers would like to thank the following for permission to reproduce pictures on these pages
T=Top, B=Bottom, L=Left, R=Right, C=Centre

www.bridgeman.co.uk/Private Collection 19;
© Bettmann/Corbis 10, © Hulton-Deutsch Collection/Corbis 15, © Michael Nicholson/Corbis 12; © Getty Images/Hulton Archive 9, 14, 18B, 21, 22, 24, 25, 29, 32, 40, 41T&B, 44, 45L, 53T&B, 58T; Illustrated London News Photo Library 45R; Mary Evans Picture Library 11T&B, 18T, 23, 27, 36, 50, 52, 58B.

Cover picture: © Hulton Deutsch Collection/Corbis

Every effort has been made to contact the holders of copyright material, but if any have been inadvertently overlooked the Publishers will be pleased to make the necessary arrangements at the first opportunity.

You might also like to visit
www.harpercollins.co.uk
The book lovers' website